Rice Bowls

My view of the world.

Rice Bowls

Excerpts from Life

By Koon Woon

Goldfish Press
Seattle

Copyright © 2018 by Koon Woon
All rights reserved

Goldfish Press
4545 42nd Avenue Southwest
Suite 211
Seattle, WA 98116-4243

Manufactured in the United States of America

ISBN-13: 978-0971259881
ISBN-10: 0971259887

Library of Congress Catalog Card Number: 2018906139

Book & Cover Design by Koon Woon

Dedication:

This book is for Susan Steiner.

ACKNOWLEDGEMENTS:

This book is supported by a generous grant from the City of Seattle's Office of Arts & Culture.

OFFICE OF ARTS & CULTURE

SEATTLE

With Special Thanks to Irene Gomez

Table of Contents

Introduction

"Rice bowl" is the expression of one's livelihood in the Chinese lingo. It means how and by what means one survives. For example, an "iron rice bowl" means a guaranteed income, meaning one's economic security. Since China was for millennia an agricultural country, rice means the substance of survival, and in the parts of China where I come from and the fact that rice is planted in the mud, a woman of "good mud" means she is winsome and fertile.

"Billy Pilgrim," in Kurt Vonnegut Jr.'s book, Slaughterhouse Five, "had become unstuck in time." He was able to go into the future and into the past quite as easily as you and I could slip into and out of our clothes. Well, actually, it was not up to him where and what epoch he would end up. It was at the whims of the Tralfamadoreans, aliens that had captured him.

In a similar way, but being stuck in time, I could not choose how things happened and what if things could have happened otherwise. I am now sixty-nine years old, living in a high rise apartment for the elderly and disabled in the bedroom community of high tech Seattle called The Junction in West Seattle. How I got from the village in China at birth to this lower middle-class neighborhood is what my story is about. But only selections will be given as life is as long as a conversation with a river; the water just ebbs on and on.

This book is multi-genre with a mixture of poems, vignettes, stories, descriptions, observations and essays that together weave the experiences of my life as a Chinese immigrant to the United States. I am of the generation 1½ , so-called for persons spending childhood in China and the formative years in the United States. Thus, I am bi-cultural. Sometimes it feels like I am a cultural ambassador, a chameleon, one tree with two birds in it singing, or in the worst case, like someone straddling the cracks of an earthquake. And so "identity" is an issue that needs constantly resolving.

This "book" isn't finished as no book is ever finished, it just gets published. It is rather a compilation of notes, poems, vignettes, and sketches. Some have appeared in journals and some in books. The unfinished quality is somehow a mirror of the author's chaotic life. It is a life that I as a person would not wish on anyone, except those who sees anything in life is worth investigating, mulling on, and chronicalizing.

Nowadays I am approaching old age and becoming more and more sedentary, and the only thing that roams around is the mind in memories. I suppose now is good of a time as any to review some of the incidents in life, hopefully to auto-correct, but if unable to improve much, I can document this for my nephews and nieces, because where I came from originally, China, the avuncular relation is very important.

I. [Some came on a slow boat from China]

The River, the Boat

When facing the sun's progress, my heart is
churned by its rays, as the Yellow River's waters are
churning ten fathoms deep,
and when I compose my life by music of moonlight,
I cannot help but think of other great rivers of the world,
and their transporting immense mountains to sea.

And when I see my face and yours in the same mirror,
I learn the blend of Arabic and South American coffees that
slowly roast our hearts with the first cup, waking us to a slight
bitterness, but coffee is coffee, black is black, pain is pain,
and life is life. So, I know the gift of your heart is long in the
preparing and my acceptance is quick in the receiving,

And so as you shower me with this great gift of monsoon rain,
my heart softens as the rice paddies are ready for planting, and
though there are leeches in the water that will steal our blood,
our crop will invariably bring us great abundance because of
your light and the power of the sun.

That the moon still can cast a cold glimmer but she alone
shivers naked in the sky and still the oceans will not freeze
and we will be seventy-seven one day, like so many lit candles
in the wind, when morning is no guarantee for the evening,
and we both know that more rains will come,
but we are also certain that as the river rises, so does our boat.

Where I Come from:

It was Oak Street in Aberdeen, then it wasn't. It was Twelve Avenue in Seattle, then it wasn't. It was Ferry Street in Eugene, Oregon, then it wasn't, etc. None of these places and more where I had lived, they were not my neighborhood, my home. I was less than a guest.

In Toishan the sun was brighter, the rain wetter, and the breeze more welcome. I was born there in a village in some southern part of China's Guangdong Province. *Big Brother Mao* was chairman. He oversaw 600 million people, most of them like me and grandma, my uncles, aunts, and cousins. We were peasants.

Wallace Stevens walked to and from work at Hartford Insurance where he was vice-president. He had diabetes and he needed the walk. While walking, he composed poems in his head.

In the village called Nan On or *Southern Peace*, I did not know what poetry was but I saw the blazing sun on the guava trees, the dogs running in the village yards, and men and women arcing in paddies planting rice.

Thomas Mann wrote exactly one page before breakfast.

I watered grandmother's gardens twice a day. These are the "wet" gardens aligned next to the village pond. I dip a spout into the water and I sprinkle it on rows of vegetables. I don't know how long this arrangement had been in place. Some things were practiced for centuries such as arranged marriages. I saw such a marriage in the next village. A bridal sedan brought the bride. It must have been thrilling for the bride as a musical troupe accompanied her to the groom's village. I have been told that my parents were married this way at age sixteen.

Where I really come from:

Note from Zembla

I am writing you from a far country where water traverses many miles of convoluted pipes and up many floors to the spigot in my room that sputters and streams this colorless liquid in two different and yet adjustable temperatures. There is also a box that televises the great leader's head, though I must say, more often than I like. People puff on short burning sticks to inhale their anguish, and often times; they imbibe a certain class of liquids that make them speak and act silly or aggressive. These people have among themselves observers called "sociologists," who are doing comparable work that I do, except, their work is called "social science," whereas mine is called "fiction."

The Proprietress of Love

"Something there is making my heart empty."
She is fond of divulging.

My Uncle pens firmly from China, "Ai mo nung tsor (love to but unable to help)." As Lorca in his somnambular ballad, "Mocito, si yo puedo, este trado estaba cerraba, per yo no soy yo, y ni mi casa es ya mi casa (If I were able, lad, this bargain would be closed. But I am no long I, nor my house is any longer my house)."

The cracks in the sidewalk are not a match for this day of thunder in the sky, the sixth day of the storm season, and the wind forebodes downed power lines, like the pain of jilted love.

She is fond of giving me her hand, when no customers are in the store and says, "Look how fast my hands are aging!" I cast a lazy glance toward the videos of love, and say, I can, I can manage you. And as she smiles, a customer walks in.

I return often when either she or I need a boost from each other.

Somewhere hidden in the city Mr. Five Willows is staring at the computer screen, with a glass of wine within reach, and as he pours from the bottle to refill the glass, a sudden downpour of rain outside. It is too early to trust the weather.

At the barbecue shop a man purchases a roast duck, cleaved and boxed by "the chop-chop man," who laments he is not an old "wah queue (long-time immigrant)." His cleaver swings up and chops down all day long, and no, this is not a persistent mirage. Someone is eating with oily lips tonight. Someone who is already fat.

The Memory of hands
(in memory of my grandmother)

I. In Water Buffalo Time

Honey-auntie collects bees in her palms:
When she says Go! they fly off to sue the flowers.
And when she says Come Back! they roll their honey-
bellies in her hand.

Uncles are in rice paddies, itching where leeches suck
their legs.

I sprinkle Grandmother's garden of bokchoy, cabbages,
and wintermelons heavy like little buddhas.

Grandmother gets wood and gossip from Firewood-auntie,
and pays her a few bronze coins to light incense.
Both women's husbands died three decades ago,
leaving them the void of Confucian hands.

At dusk my grandmother trots out in her bound feet to retrieve
the drying vegetables hung on a bamboo pole like the character
jen (people).

The sun drops behind the last rice paddy
as the water buffalo sinks in the village pond,
dropping dung for black shrimps.
And at last Grandmother draws the mosquito net
in the lychee-pit night.

II. Sampan

A journey in yellow water. I am sick
and Grandmother tells me to think of not moving.
Think of a place far away like Gimshan, she says

Do not move against the river and you will be still.
Don't resist the womb's muscles to deliver you.
Your head was so big we used forceps,
and now you are a cavern
for three bowls of rice and pigs' feet stewed in rice vinegar!

Grandmother is not moving although the boat moves.
She tells me to think of lemon.

The boatman, pushing the river bottom with his long bamboo
pole,
carries all the land he cares for in his sampan.
As I become better, I awe at his calves.

The river I know must have fish.
The fish must look up at the shadow that moves.
The fish move in a moving river,
but I am still because Grandmother is still.

We are leaving the village for Canton.
The chrysanthemums are in bloom just now,
and Gimshan is where I must soon go.

III. The World's Longest Alley

For a snip of cloth Grandmother took my hand
and led me through bicycle-laden streets,
past shoppers by fours, past wine and vinegar stores.
Buses overtook us.
And finally, walking as far as three rolls
of cloth would unroll,
we arrived at the entrance of the world's longest alley,
where vendors on both sides set up
painted fans, brilliantly glazed pottery,
and cloth of every color
as they haggled with shoppers,
squeezing the alley like a tourniquet on a blood vessel.

Grandmother: "The five colors blind the eye!"
But she doesn't heed Lao Tsu and slides her fingers
on the rolls of exquisite cloth.
We hear it is exported.

But there are no candy vendors, though there's a man
who has taught his monkey to beg with a tipped hat.
The alley is long as a conversation with a river.
In the colorful blur, she assents to an ice-cream bar.
I am then happy for coming along,
for the first time I see
Grandmother as a maiden of sixteen,
her young eyes dazzled by the dowry of cloth.

IV. The Memory of Hands

If you fold a piece of paper once, then unfold it,
it will tend toward the folded position. That's because
the paper has "memory."

The memory of hands, of ancient vine.
My monsoon eyes, my face, tilled by fingers.
A chicken plucked gently naked.
Hands, unable to sign a legal signature,
close the fan,
and draw the mosquito net.

At the Hong Kong International Airport, I took a mental
photograph of my grandmother. A young girl wrings free of
her mother's hand and runs along, laughing.

Her index finger wrote a whorl on my back to designate an ox.
My hands, curved upward to suggest valleys of space,
would squeeze water,
would cling to ancient vine,
would throw

a marble across the river.

The loudspeaker announces, announces last call, last call.
Third-aunt says hurry, hurry, or you will miss your future.

The past folds up like an origami bird,
will not dissolve like candy.
Grapes cling to the vine, hands weave bamboo baskets,
hands supplicate and light incense,
Buddha holds her in his palm.
I fold paper for hands of ancient vine,
hands that couldn't come along.
And hands will open gates if I should return.

"Gimshan" is Cantonese for America, literally "Golden Mountain".

Father & Son

A father's hand covers a son's hand, and his length laps the son's. He is stirring a wok of chop suey in the Chinese-American restaurant kitchen. The son, in the slow hours, in a waiter's yellow jacket, secretly hopes that business will never get better, that the quarrelsome customers will stay home and cook their own hamburgers and spaghetti, drink Coke instead of tea, as he, in the fugitive hours, ponders the texts of Ludwig von Wittgenstein, Hughes and Creswell, and Immanuel Kant thrown in for good measure. He is home from the erudite university for the summer, in the folds of the reversed prejudices of his Chinese-American family; however, it must be said, the father does not confuse chop suey with potato salad, mortgage with taxes, firemen with insurance salesmen, for dealing with various realities he has become to a degree objective.

While the son seeks truths that last longer than the life of a restaurant in a small town, or longer than all the McDonalds in all towns, but alas, he will find in books only in the phantom hours, when traffic has slowed to a halt, when husbands are exhausted from work at pulp and shingle mills, tired from demanding wives and unruly children, only small towns facts that go unrecorded, such as the locals betting with the local bookies on Team A, and his truths in books that exist only in books, giving that he wears thick glasses. And he is all too busy thinking that he is thinking and all the while never thinks about what his father is thinking.

The son doesn't imagine the day will come years after his father's death, when a long-trusted family friend will casually say, "You walk like your father now." Now, suddenly like a cloudless day in October, he is free, free from the tangles of bickering philosophers, the webs of literary jealousy, when he thinks of his late father, how his back had, in the span of forty years bending over the wok, had become a bow, like the bow of William Tell, and he shall take his children and grandchildren like he would take and position arrows, set them firmly in place, and shoot them, shoot them toward the stars...

Elemental

Today late in March
I walked to the deli
in the inner-city
The cold wind elemental
Nostalgic
There was a time when
all comforts I had was to let
the blank page reflect me
while paranoia rushed about
the tenement room with cars
going up Jackson Street gleaming
aggression

While I play postal – chess with an uncle
an ocean away
and his face is on every stamp
Wisdom hidden like three – leaved
clovers among the weeds.

How long before I feel secure
in early lessons,
the bird songs,
the village mornings,
the simple joys
from water,
the warm breath of wind
and crickets in the evening,
moon – lit and stars ample.

Going into old – age
in old ways –
fearless and
with grace.

A Smoke Break at the Nuclear Command

We multitask chop, grill, wok, and pickle.
They are fickle, can come all hours, drunk,
after sex, before meetings, during greetings;
hucksters, gangsters, no telling who wants what
stir-fried, steamed rock cod with its head and bulbous eyes.
My father at the meat block hacks spareribs, carves bone from
chicken, minces onions, six sons chow the mein, French-fry the
sausages, whip the gravy, beat the eggs until you can fool the young
into thinking that's sperm yanked from a calf.
Smoke signals say the pork chops are burnt,
the white sauce turning yellow and the waitresses ladle the soup.
Sounds like feeding at the zoo. Chopsticks tingle from a corner
booth.

On and on motors start and stop, door open and shut, ice water
set down as menus are tossed. You need a minute? Mom is helping
the girls to wash glasses and tea pots. It would be sinful to run out of
hot mustard during the rush.
My father drinks my coffee and I smoke his Marlboro,
Two cowboys in cattle drive fending off rustlers, and damn!
The waitress says that the women's toilet has overflowed!

We are going to go fishing as soon as our mental breakdowns are
over with.
And we are going to take a smoke break from the nuclear command.
Just then a party of 12 comes in – well, put two tables together,
like a man joining a woman, the yin and yang, and kids with yo-yo's.
We are family doing family business, money for school books,
Mom's dentures.

When Kafka Is Unhappy...
카프카는 우울할 때...

When Kafka is unhappy, he paces about his room in the rooming house known as
"The Castle." He shares the carpet with a little girl ghost as she runs back and forth, stepping
over his slippers, humming Leonard Cohen's tune "Suzanne," and ignores the writer/lawyer altogether..
She has a mind of her own, thinks Franz. *But I have to keep my windows shut so that caterpillars can't get in here and eat what's left of my bagel with cream cheese.*
카프카는 우울할 때, '성'이라고 알려진 그의 하숙집 방을 배회합니다. 그의 방에는 그와 카펫을 함께 사용하는 어린 소녀 유령 아이가 있죠. 그 아이는 이리 저리 달리고 그의 슬리퍼를 밟으며 레오나드 코헨의 "수잔"을 읊조리면서 그 작가/변호사는 무시해버립니다.
프란츠는 생각하죠. 그녀는 그녀만의 세계가 있구나. 하지만 난 애벌레가 들어오지 못하도록 내 창문을 닫아야만 해 그리고 남은 베이글을 크림 치즈와 함께 먹어야지.

Being a lawyer and working for the Disability Compensation Bureau, Kafka sees many people down on their luck. One mistake in the workplace can cost you your hand or an arm. And a ton of bricks can fall on you at the factory if the forklift guy isn't looking out for you. And so you join the union. Safety in numbers.
장애인 보상 조합 사무실에서 일하는 변호사, 카프카는 많은 사람들이 곤경에 처하는 것을 발견하곤 하죠. 일터에서의 한 번의 실수가 엄청난 대가를 치르게 되기도 하고, 지게차 운전자가 조심스럽게 주변을 살피지 않는다면, 공장에서 일하는 이들에게 벽돌이 떨어질 수도 있습니다. 그러면 그들은 이 안전 조합에 가입하게 되지요.

The other day Max Brod came over and wanted to be literary executor of his novels. Franz is not so eager to publish his works in his lifetime. "Just think, my dear Franz, with your clean prose, elegant and Spartan, and your ideas, what ideas! How can you deprive the world of this literary feast?" Franz remains mum. He is afraid that success, if it does come, would spoil his anonymity and even

misrepresent him. *I wrote because of these maddening ideas, and in no way am
I going to betray my little girl ghost in my room.*
　이전날 맥스 브로드씨가 찾아와서 그의 소설의 출판
관리자가 되고 싶다고 말했었죠. 프란츠씨는 그가 살아있는
동안에는 그의 소설을 출판하고 싶지 않은데도 말이죠.
"친애하는 프란츠씨, 한 번만 고민해주세요. 당신의 깔끔한 글,
우아하고 절제된 생각들, 이 얼마나 멋진 일입니까? 어떻게
당신은 이런 멋진 문학의 향연을 포기할 수가 있죠?"
프란츠씨는 잠자코 있었지요. 그는 성공을 두려워합니다. 그가
성공한다면, 그의 익명성을 망칠 것이고 심지어 그를 잘못
표현할지도 모릅니다. *나는 미칠 것 같은 내 생각들을 표현할
뿐이고 그것은 내 방의 작은 소녀 유령 아이를 배신하는
어떠한 것도 아니야.*

Kafka does lament that the door of his room leads to the
communal den. And when he leaves or comes he needs to see other
boarders eating at the communal table where Joe leans his bicycles.
He is careful not to let the girl ghost out of the room. He always
worry that she is too thin and has an eating disorder. He usually buys
a loaf of bread, cheese, and liverwurst and hides it in his lawyer's bag
for the girl. She never touches the food.
　카프카는 그의 방문이 하숙집 중앙 쪽으로 연결되어 있다는
것이 애통할 뿐입니다. 그가 들어오거나 나갈 때마다
하숙인들이 공동 테이블에 앉아서 먹는 것을 보아야만 하고
거기엔 조가 그의 자전거에 몸을 기대어 있곤 하지요. 그는 늘
소녀 유령이 방에서 나가지 않도록 조심합니다. 그는 그녀가
너무 말랐고 식이 장애가 있다고 생각하죠. 그는 자주 그 소녀
유령을 위하여 빵 한 조각, 치즈, 소시지를 그의 가방에
숨겨두곤 하죠. 그렇지만 그녀는 그 음식에는 손도 대지
않습니다.

And so Kafka ends up eating what he brought for the girl ghost,
and thinks about justice in a small way. It is overly misrepresented, he
thinks. We lock ghosts up and they haven't done us the least harm.
He thought about a passage from Leonard Cohen's early poems, "I
wonder, when I look out the window of the furnished room, how
many people are looking back at me?"
　결국, 카프카는 소녀 유령을 위하여 가져온 음식을
먹으면서 정의라는 것에 대하여 잠시 고민해봅니다. 그는
정의가 너무나 잘못 표현되었다고 생각하죠. 우리는 유령을

가두지만 그 유령들이 우리에게 해악을 끼친 건 하나도
없다고. 그는 레오나드 코헨의 초기 작품인 시詩 "나에게
알려다오, 가구가 딸려있는 내 방 창문가에서 밖을 바라볼 때,
가던 길 뒤돌아 나에게 손짓해 줄 이가 몇이나 되는지." 한
구절을 생각합니다.

Kafka kept on writing throughout the night. He knows that on a cold, cold day, his manuscript can make a pale fire. The thought of that makes him feel warm. He ignores the little girl ghost as she raced up and down the carpet. Writing was his real job.

카프카는 밤새도록 글을 씁니다. 그는 그의 글이 창백한
불꽃을 지필 수 있다는 것을 알죠. 그를 따뜻하게 만드는 생각.
작은 소녀 유령이 위 아래를 뛰어다니지만 그는 무시합니다.
글을 쓰는 것이 그의 진정한 직업이니까요.

Translated into Korean by Lisa MN Yoon LES
October 3, 2015

A Moment in my rented room

I sometimes think of myself as an astronaut
In my compact, rented room and look upon the bookshelf
With its deep mathematics books for deeper space
As from a voyage one cannot return.
Then multiply by several million men who cannot marry,
Men who cannot own homes, or work, or go to college.

This is almost equal to the space effort.
But why all that money? I can go to Pluto by just
Being in a bad mood.
Sometimes I think of the loneliness of deep space
In my rented room. The neighbors have busily gone off
To Epsilon Centauri or Galaxy X-2137 or to the 7 Eleven.
Sometimes I look at my 16-oz. jar of coffee; I know
What the minimum daily requirements are. Cybernetics
Steers me to avoid collisions with black holes or stars,
And my hot plate sustains me with pinto beans and bacon rinds,
And on my mini-stereo, always the Blue Danube.
It is rainy today. My room is a bastion. I am filing
The sparse bars of prison. I am building a mental atom bomb.
I am designing spaceships. Multiply this by several millions.

However Deep the Night I Expect Morning

Fog rolls into the valley, rolls
Where my mind goes into the evening,
As the rhythm of city syncopates my walk,
The roar of jets, the whisper of beggars,
Parks have their statues

In this city I know
Know where to find the best soup,
Where often the bands play the pigeons flock
Above heads of idols and unknown heroes
Not far from my tenement above Stockton and Vallejo;
I play Go from a book.

Rinds of light and rain fall silently
Equally on door knobs of silver or copper
This town dreams are altered by Andy and Val
Fight domestic while mice noisily cum
They do not expect morning

I think of crimson electric when morning sun rises
Arriving like a Chagall painting
A man floats up to kiss a woman from the Bolshoi Ballet

I am writing to you as I do, ever so remorseful
The window sill announces there is rain outside
But your purring has begun here in pulses of 8 to 80
As you break night once more and again
I write to you as I do and writing as you yourself do

On onion skin the lightest of verse
The lightest of verse, the lightest of verse

A Drive to Nowhere

Like I would just jump into the car; it was variously a '55 Plymouth, a '61 Comet, or a '68 Plymouth again. Where would I go? There was no one I know on a Saturday. The weekends, the dreaded weekends. My search for psychic sustenance begins with those fifty mile drives to nowhere.

The family restaurant would be busy on the weekends. I would need to work until three in the morning on both Friday and Saturday nights, amid the grease vapors and the clanging of the wok, steam from the noodle vat and the steam table. I was eighteen and still a senior in high school in the coastal town of Aberdeen, Washington. These are the towns that the freeway missed in Richard Hugo's poetry. The rain was melancholic and it drip and slanted all day, and I was trapped being "Number-One-Son" of a Chinese immigrant family, born to Kim and Bill who operated the Hong Kong Café on Simpson Avenue which was on the Highway 101 as it slices through the logging town of Aberdeen, where logging trucks carried the long logs with dancing red flags on them to warn the drives behind it. This road goes up to Forks, Washington and eventually to Port Angeles as it looped around the Olympia Peninsula. And going south, the same two –lane road would lead to Pacifica, California.

I worked variously as waiter, cook, and occasionally manager. Except for work and study, I was lonely and alone. I was so lonely that I enjoyed reading Silas Marner in my room during the holidays of Thanksgiving and Christmas, the only two days that we closed the café. My parents had undergone the world-wide Depression in their youth in China and then the Sino-Japanese War. I was so lonely that the book on the back seat of my car, Eleven Kinds of Loneliness was actually a good dialogue with an imaginary companion. I knew the writer in the sense that he knew me, he knew my loneliness. It was a small town, and there were few minorities in it. There was a black janitor at the Smoke Shop Café, owned by the mayor. I suspect that he was there for a reason, just like the only black student at the local Grays Harbor College was a football player. The black janitor seemed to recede into the wood panels of the café dining room as he mopped it during idle hours.

I remember I kept on filling the coffee cup of the girl with the dark Spanish eyes that came alone or with her sister, mostly alone. She drank her coffee black and I was the awkward waiter in the slow hours of the afternoon. She and I never chit-chat and I never learned her name, but somehow once I summoned the nerve to asked her whether she lived at home. She said she lived away from home alone and as long as she doesn't get into trouble, it was OK with her mom. She was a year older and had dropped out of high school. I was also a part-time worker at the Aberdeen post office and I drove the truck two hours in the morning and two hours in the afternoon picking up mail from street boxes. And on Saturday, I had the downtown walking route. I had a regulation uniform on, and I felt like a worker, a government worker.

The way out of town was a windy road, evergreens on both sides, a monotonous green with firs shooting up 30 to 40 feet. These were new growth and I was a fourth generation immigrant to these parts of lands. I was wondering how far I could go and how high I could rise. But all I could envision was driving a modest car to work at Boeing and perhaps have a son and a daughter and live again in a modest house, befitting of an electrical engineer. Everybody in high school said I could have become whatever I wanted to.

I didn't go that far, I drove to Ocean Shores and back then in 1968 it was only one street along the beach front with the burr of the crabgrass waving in the wind. There were summer homes that people did not live in during the winter. It was fog and winter mists as described in Ken Kesey's novel <u>Sometimes a Great Notion.</u> He was talking about the roads in Oregon. Here the crabgrass rose from the sand, an occasional gull, and the steady sloshing waves greeted my loneliness, and I encounter no other cars.

In Water Buffalo time

The water buffalo is a black boulder around which white
Butterflies flit, controlling the image of my village.
It is four pillars holding up a shrine topped by Attila's head.
Slapping its paintbrush tail, sure-footed, it advances
Slowly, not impressed by dynastic inventions of paper, compass,
and gunpowder,
Not by imperial vassals intoxicating concubines with plum wine.
This working philosophic benign beast of the East, a prince
Meditating on plum blossoms while the kingdom is overrun
By brigands no different than soldiers.
It sinks its head into the grass on the perimeter of the village
Pond where daggers of carp and dace rip his shadow on the water,
Where black shrimp and loaches scout the bottom
And snails cling to slate banks.

In earliest mornings, I woke to the village dialect jostling
In my head like cauliflowers sizzling in sesame oil
In the wok, like chatty sparrows in the yung tree,
Like cicadas in bamboo groves, like buckets splashing
Into the village well. I heard the drinking song of the men
In the village yard the night before. With bamboo pipes
And a bucket of rice wine, they had sung.

"Heavy, heavy, the dew lies over the clovers.
Bring, bring out flasks of silver.
Merry, merry under a dome of stars.
But soon, too soon this night will be over..."

Voices taut, frog drums deep as rice paddies.
But I dreamt a deeper voice, my father's pales in comparison.

It's hinted by Gungfu drums, bellow of water buffalo, a racine
fissure.
It was as proclaimed by Lu Hsun, "In the stillness of mountains,
Hear the peal of thunder." But when I woke, the dew was gone.
A shaft of sunlight fell on my childhood slate.

My sister renews the Ming vase with fresh pussy willows.
Grandmother steams rice, and the chicken sits on a new egg.
I drink tea from the sprout while my sister redoes my shoelaces.
Off to school 3 li away, trotting on village pond banks
And collecting schoolmates in the morning haze.
When I see a water snake swimming on the lotus pond,
I déjà vu Narcissus lost his life. His gifts came early
And ours not at all. We are the contingent of zodiac animals
Off to seek Buddha: the horse, the rabbit, the tiger, the rooster...
The ox trots out first, faithful, steadfast, but when he
Arrives, the rat on his back jumps off
And gets to Buddha first.

I often meditate at the pond near the school,
Watching the soft, thin legs of the praying mantis
Subdue a bug in full armor, seeing it as the monks did
In Shaolin Temple 500 years before. Other masters studied
The movements of cranes, eagles, and birds fighting with snakes.
Li Po, our legendary poet, in 700 A.D., perfected
The Drunkard's Style of Gungfu, which bewilders
The opponent with fluid but erratic movements.

When my little friends mocked me for my seriousness,
Our teacher, under the shade of the yung tree bursting with berries,
Told us Meng-Tse had dreamed he was a butterfly
Dreaming it was a man. I was confused, in a house

Of mirrors, and thought existence is mutual illusion.
Would I cease to exist if I didn't think of my dog
Who thinks of me? My little friends made faces at me.

New Year comes to the village banging a gong
And exploding demon-chasing firecrackers. And lucky money.
But the village recedes away like the galaxies. In these
Thirty years what will not change in form or utility
Except art for its own sake?
Heraclitus says I can't cross the same river twice.
Einstein says if I must I can go to the future, but never to the past.
But surely as long as one water buffalo is fanned by
The evening breeze, the village is there like the smile of the Cheshire
Cat
And exists in the Platonic world; all else is an approximation.

Sunflowers, yellow and white chrysanthemums, lychees,
Girls' red cheeks, dew-moist wintermelon little buddhas
In the gardens. Robins, beetles, and cicadas sing my way
To my uncle's village. He rises and his wife burns incense.
He clears the abacus with one motion and teaches me the rhymes
One chants to enable the fingers to go faster than the brain.

He is a wine merchant steeped in Confucius.
Where would a woman wash her husband's clothes
If not at the river by the ancestral shrine?
What part of the chicken to give to the nephew if not the drumstick?
And how else to measure but by exact yards and inches?
He has many children but there is no unnecessary noise.

I forage the pine hills behind his house as a bandit.
The turpentine from the virgin pines makes me dizzy.
The wood is kept as furniture for newlyweds.

I play until I fear real bandits will come
When the sky is devout with thousands of incense tips.

But surely memory is selective. I don't remember not having
My mother's milk, only the quarrels with village women
My mother's age. I don't remember three generations of a family
Taken by dysentery, just the bitter cod liver oil
My grandmother spooned me.
I don't remember my cold little toe except that cloth was allotted
Only once a year, and only in black or blue.
I don't remember famines, just the human chain formed
To relay water to the stricken rice paddies,
Where the leeches had dehydrated.

Still, village girls marry as soon as the dew evaporates
From the corn. The mulberry was for jumping into the village pond.
What China had, we had. And when it was all quiet,
The sunflowers so turned. The papayas got fat and golden,
And peasants trotted out with hoes and straw hats.
It is quiet in the garden where I fish in the pond.
Peas incubate in pods, the lettuce full and clean,
And ladybugs monitor the gardens
To make sure this is the order of things
Before the invention of mail delivery.

In the semi-tropical evening, pink clouds race and diffuse
Like the colors and textures of my jade bracelet.
The water buffalo is led into the dusty village yard,
Mud-caked on its loins, distracted by my dog cutting
Across its path. He collects his primeval motions into shape,
Shakes his Hegelian head, exhales, slaps his paintbrush tail,
Lapses into a revelry, and goes into internal monologue:

O beast I am, humble beast.
Some man, he must have been an emperor,
Or the son of such an emperor, said, "The Original Son
Is the mother of the universe, the sword that divines light
From chaos, the mother of all things..."
The sun atop the tree is East.
The mountains seek comfort in the hills, the hills seek
Rest in the valleys, and the valleys beget rivers.
The mountain cat descends into the lowlands
And the field mice look up for hawks
And the darkening earth looks for the moon...

And loving the grasses as I have for thirty years,
First owned by one man, then by his son,
While the mountains are unvarying,
With mud caked on my loins, trudging the maze of rice fields,
A black dot against unvarying mountains,
The soil furls, my eyebrows moisten, the bittersweet song
Of my master, himself deep in mud, the fury of work,
Calculating how many bowls of rice the harvest will give.

A beast is not able to calculate mous, catties, and grains.
Work begins when the monsoons recede. In the evening,
When I am sufficiently grazed, I sink into the village pond
And drop dung for black shrimp...

Yet a man, with all his skill on an abacus, is afraid
Of things he cannot see. The man and his family
Are afraid of dark, gloomy gods handed down to them
And buy copious amounts of incense and charms.
My mother, whose teats I suckled for only a brief while,
Gave me no such gods of thunder to fear.

I don't even fear tigers. A man is cursed with worry:
Thieves because he has too much, fires because he is careless,
And ghosts because he offends others.
But I, with the gold-pleated sky for a blanket,
Sweet-smelling rice straw for a bed, a breeze from the river,
I have recompense for my toil, with the village symphony
Of crickets, cicadas, and bullfrogs,
I shall say beasthood is as good as Buddhahood.

I conjecture a water buffalo constellation in another galaxy,
A real spirit, not a tattered array of dying stars,
A form but not only a form.
Up in heaven, my soul mate has no ring pierced
Through his elegant nose and no harness to shackle him down.
And here below, if beasts can speak, we will form quorums
And overthrow empires by a conspiracy of tails.

But alas, nature gives us no such voice or equipment
Just a reluctant compliance to serve.
Though our masters in turn fear the tax collectors,
It is we who are sold, exchanged, or placed on the chopping block.
We do not think? No!
Our lack is that our intelligence is not equal to our strength.

The beast is weary, is led by a boy to a bed of straw.
Inside our house, in the kerosene lamplight,
My sister undoes her ponytail, which a while ago was a bowstring
Back from a political meeting, she says tractors will come
To our village. When electric lamps light up the village yard,
She says, ghosts will be gone.
Grandmother, with her feet bound in the last dynasty, will see
New light with her old eyes.

She gives me crackers and tea, and draws the mosquito net.
I hear a faint moan from the water buffalo.
He too will be liberated.
Though the past is solipsistic, its existence requiring
A mind to behold it, childhood writes indelibly
A million dollar check into life.
Dragonflies hover over chrysanthemums
Like helicopters over a burning forest.
Bananas and grapes bunch together like families.

Women splash buckets into the well.
I look for the faint prints of water buffalo.
The water buffalo got old and died.
It was shared by the whole village,
Lucky money for a calf conscripted.
A sad note crept into the men's drinking songs,
But not for long, with rice wine they sang
Again of subduing tigers and the various calamities
From the beginning of time.
On my childhood slate were drawings of chickens, mulberries,
And numerals from Arabia.
Then I learned how to write the characters "water buffalo."

An Old hotel dweller

Smoke detectors page me down these halls.
Cooking pork snouts no doubt, my arthritic bones
rickshaw me down scented rugs to the toilet stall.
Old San likes to read old papers and fart alone.
First the check is late, then mice noisily came,
and the daughter moves to another town.
Old photographs and plaster can but come down.
When Old San sneezes, he discovers he's lame
and eight flights of stairs lead down to the snow.
The women in the washroom will only say
may the Virgin Mary give us more hot water.
Old age is like this, Old San has been told.
But I am still living, though life is a bother.
I hope I won't be a putrefying mess on the next rent day.

They come at me with hatchets

I had this horrendous nightmare that my father is really a vampire, the lead vampire and I was infected! In the village we attend Party meetings and toil in the rice paddies but when we sleep, our bodies open with a thousand sores, and we need blood to coat our sores. Nowhere is this found in Party Literature and we are forbidden to speak, write or even think of it.

At day, everyone greet us deferentially, but it is only due to the fact that the Party had appointed us, and if they know that we suck their blood with our phantom proboscis while they sleep, they would tear us apart limb by limb.

In the morning everyone wakes with a sense of violation. They have been drained of their blood and robbed of their strength. This is the way we collect "taxes" for the Party, and one may call it the Old-Fashioned Way, the way that cannot be told, but the way that is the way...

My father tells me never to tell. When by chance his mosquito avatar meets with mine sucking the same victim, he gives me the skull and he takes the thigh. "I get the fat and you get the bone," he says. I oblige because I am a dutiful son. I help my father planting rice as well as harvesting it in the rice paddies. But we are not fat from rice; we are fat from others' blood. If they know that I am writing this down, the victims and even my father would come at me in the daylight with hatchets...

Cityscape with Solitary Figure

Not a sparrow is yet up, nor the milk trucks.
Even to malign him, the street lamps are frugal.
He who is under the shadow of the building, a deeper shadow.
He who hauls his house on his back.
Must we avoid acknowledging him?
He whose going does not make an arriving.

In the darkness he is white, brown, or black –
No one can tell or would tell.
He knows the various grids of the city and how far
Into the morning before he can get a free cup of coffee.
The park benches are partitioned
And signs saying no camping. What a life!

Formerly there was shelter from the rain
Beneath the bridge, but the stench of graffiti
Forced him to brightly-lit doorways before dawn.
Merchant-hired security sweeps him
Up in the morning and he goes as a lump
Of coal in the snow, going just for the sake of go.

Two birds, one tree

Two birds, one tree
Two birds in one tree argue
over its span, its symbolic reach,
the meaning of it all, the seeds,
the fallen leaves,
finalized by gravity.

Two men in one boat discuss
the ripples on water,
the bob and the line,
the murky depths,
in fathoms beneath.

Four creatures thus converse
across the elements of
wind and water,
growth and grossness
of life and its demise.

That the wind may blow
and water perturbate,
that men and birds imitate
the world's inadvertent sounds,
as time is lost and we lose ground
 the note and the nodes,
its liveliness casually found.

The Old House on Bay Avenue

I slept in the anteroom because the bed was there and early in the morning while still in bed the freight train would rattle by just across the dirt fields, cycloned by blackberry brambles. When the roar of the engines died, I would gradually hear robins or sparrows chirping and singing. Those days I was 21 and 22 and I didn't need coffee or strong tea to wake up yet and I would linger in bed relishing the morning deliciously because my strength was still in my brain and my eyes and limbs were good and young though my loins were still virgin and it was to be another 3 years before I have my first sexual experience with an older married woman from Aberdeen.

For now group and ring theory filled my head and no one has licked the Pacific Rim of my cock yet. I had many women and girl friends and I mean just Platonic friends because I made friends easily and I was not a threat to them; I did not demand sex, though a few would really want to initiate me. I was that shy. I remember Reed who taught me how to kiss in my car before I went down to Eugene to attend the University of Oregon and maybe the trouble was that it had started with Eileen. I will talk about that in a little bit. That was my first frost in the telephone booth, but in retrospect, I still love her, because she came back to me twenty years later and made it up to me.

Well, let me continue with the story on Bay Avenue then. More than anything it was a time of reading. In the summer I worked for Kerns Desoto furniture factory, a mill just a few blocks down in Hoquiam. There was not much to say about that. It was just a summer job and all they demanded was that I didn't eat in the lunch room because there were a couple of girls worked there in the wood lathes and they liked me or I mean they probably just looked at me and found me a Chinese curio, and so the red necks gave me these mean stares. The tension was so thick that I went outside and leaned about the building with its weeds and wild flowers and all to eat my sandwich and apple by myself. Nobody spoke to me and I didn't give a shit. I paid my union dues and they needed some robot to sort the wood as it came out of the saw. I discarded the pieces with the worm holes and stacked the good pieces on a pallet eight hours a day. And when I went home I took a short nap with the sawdust still in my lungs and then my brain was so clear that I read Herstein's Introduction to Abstract Algebra like it was nobody's business. How I loved that mathematical realm then.

On Saturday mornings I would drive to the Highway Grocery early in the morning and get a bottle of Mogen David blackberry wine and a yellow pad of legal paper and tried to write something. That summer when I was twenty-two I bought a Writer's Market and daydreamed that someday I will be a writer. But all I need essentially was to drink enough blackberry wine so that I felt mellow enough so that went the emerald light flooded through the bedroom window (I had moved into the back bedroom by then; it was a two-bedroom house), the unnamed tree in the backyard with its foliage and closure silhouetted itself upon the window I was transported to leagues under the sea. The world was dense and its mysteries began to beckon to me. I had also studied philosophy with John Wisdom by this time. But I didn't know how to write worth beans. But at least in a small town, I was not anomic. I was the son of Bill and Kim Woon, restaurant owners of the Hong Kong Café on Simpson Avenue. Everyone called them Mamason and Papason. But they were neither. They are as Chinese as Chinese can be, for those who know the difference between Chinese and Japanese. I was the Hong Kong Kid, as known to Dixie Wilcox' parents. Dixie and I were secretly in love, but neither one of us made any attempt to make it happen in the real world. Later when I worked for the Aberdeen Post Office, I could have asked Dixie out for a date, but I was like a sojourner in a temporary land. I never felt I belonged. The freight train was always going by and it never stops and I sometimes fancy that hoboes were on it wishing they could get off and I wished that I was on it – with destination Bangor Maine. What were those days like? I was lonely enough to fly a kite or drive fifty miles to nowhere. I particularly liked to drive to Ocean Shores and drive along the dunes with its winter crabgrass. Seagulls flapping in the ocean wind and don't know how I was ever going to break out of my mode. On weekdays there was high school with the unspoken inevitable goal of college and to take up a practical degree such as electrical engineering. In fact, as I drive along the road I could vaguely envision myself living somewhere south of Seattle and driving a modest car to work each morning, and that eventually I will have a house of my own and perhaps the sociological prediction of

2.3 children. But what would I do for fun? Will I wash my car everyday and pull weeds in the garden? Will my wife be an "introduced" bride from Hong Kong? Will my parents allow a white girl? But the key was to get good grades, and work after school at the family café. Late at night after homework is finished, I allowed myself a chess problem to analyze from my Chess Made Simple book. I also had a Shakespeare Made Simple book. Maybe I should have purchased a Simple Simon Made Simple book also. That was my one luxury. I could afford books. This poor habit will continue to grow late into life so that I will have books that couldn't understand at all but they do look very impressive in my bookshelf.

Fat Aunt

He rang the doorbell hard. Eventually a woman pushed the door curtain a crack and looked out. Opening the door, she spoke, "You here already? Where is luggage?" He looked at her short rotund body in sweats, her face is catfish-like; she is shorter and fatter than he remembers of her seven years ago.

"It is at the Greyhound station," he answered her question almost involuntarily.

"So, if you don't like Fat Aunt, you just go back to Aberdeen, eh?" Expecting no answer, she tells him to follow her upstairs. "Be careful of Buddha figurines on steps," she admonishes, "they worth money." He made a mental image of someone escaping a fire and tumbling down the stairs because of tripping over the figurines. *Money can cost you your life,* he thought to himself.

Two weeks earlier in Seattle he got a call from his father telling him of his cousin Martin's funeral. His father told him to come home immediately. He took the Greyhound home. His father told him what had happened.

"Martin got out of corrections, found his girl friend shacking up with a Wah Ching," his father begins to relate what he had heard from the Old Guy Benny. Apparently, Benny went down to San Francisco and questioned the guy who killed Martin. Martin had in a fit of jealousy climbed through his rival's window at night armed with a knife. As he approached the sleeping couple, his ex-girlfriend screamed. The new lover grabbed his gun from under his pillow and shot Martin in the neck. Martin kept coming. The new boyfriend shot him again in the neck. Incredible as it seemed, Martin was still upright and kept coming. Two more rapid shots to the neck finally put him down. Benny told his father, "It was self-defense. There is nothing we can do."

His father then said, "You go and keep your Aunt company. She is lonely now her youngest son died."
So, he came to stay with his Aunt as a matter of family obligation. Fat Aunt put him in Martin's room.

The minute he stepped into Martin's room, he had a peculiar sense that it reeked of hyper-masculinity.

In the semi-darkness the first thing he noticed was a black panther figurine on the dresser, a stack of Hustler on the foot of the bed and a Bruce Lee poster with chucks on the wall. But he was so tired he immediately crashed onto the bed and slept.

In the middle of the night, Fat Aunt roused him from his sleep. "I want you make phone call for me to Hong Kong," Fat Aunt ordered, "It is mid afternoon there now and I am looking for a boy to claim for a godson so he keep Martin's memory alive." Fat Aunt was all business, like the boss of two sweatshops she was. The nephew had spent some time in Hong Kong and knew that it was "funny business." Nevertheless, he dialed the number Fat Aunt gave him and handed the phone over to her.

"You go back to Aberdeen now and go back school in Seattle. I don't need you now. I will have someone honor memory of my son. Since the nephew was born in China, he knew something was in the works but he doesn't ask. He is a mathematics student. And he is also a philosophy student. He quoted Wittgenstein to himself, "Whereof one can speak, thereof must one speak clearly, and whereof one cannot speak, thereof must one remain silent. *All I know is that it costs money to make a telephone call to Hong Kong,* he thought to himself, *and all I did was to dial a number which I knew nothing about.*

Cold Stones

Would copper coins and amulets
from the Sung Dynasty
dispel these ghosts of regret!
We sat, face to face,
at a tea-house in Tien-An.
I call upon your name,
the old man from Nan-On.
Perhaps one should say:
"This tea comes from the high hills of..."
Or perhaps,
"This tea cup is an old relic..."
We reach into our pockets to find words
but only possess
cold stones.
The cups are emptied
and emptied again,
with the rapidity of
a school boy rattling off
the names of the dynasties.
We are old men, forever parting,
never joining.
This is the schism:
not by waters and not by years,
but by glances that implore
and by words that fail us.
When we reach into our pockets
for something to give --
cold stones.
Soul to soul, we had never met.
Our little wars had drawn us together.
Now there is peace over the hills.

Now peasants are rebuilding huts.
Can we now repair ourselves?
Or must we, like condemned men,
carry cold stones in our pockets?

Starting the day

Barely awake, I pulled the shade. It was a pristine day out, in that the blackberry brambles were so real in the emerald light, dew drops on them, with the symmetry of quadratic curves, and so I turned from being a number cruncher to a wordsmith; either way, I was going to penetrate the ordinary.

How Zen-like when the world holds still and you can peel it layer by layer until naked existence remains. Then a freight train rumbles across the dirt field, beyond the children's playground, beyond the pipeline, and already there was glory in the morning flowers. It was summer in Aberdeen on Bay Avenue.

I am a being in the world. I had come with a set of baggage but I must not lose sight of them. I can travel all day in my mind and travel light and far, rounding the curves of infinity, only to come back to the familiar. The familiar was sparrows and robins. But once I saw a blue jay and that was truly a lucky day.

I was twenty-four and it was a Saturday morning. I hurriedly got up and wrote longhand on a legal pad. I was not a lawyer but nevertheless I sought to write clearly and economically. Papers were cheap and so were pens, but my time was ticking and what was lost can never return. However, when I was that young no one thought of alerting me. They had their own stakes to harvest, so they planned. I was still starry eyed and I purchased a Writers' Market, and a day old donut and a Styrofoam of cold coffee were enough to kindle my hopes.

Weekdays I worked for the Kerns DeSoto furniture factory. The wood comes out of the saw at a rate that the feeder guy controls on the other end. I have seconds to reject the blemished and worm-holed pieces onto the conveyor belt and they are carried to the "hog" where they are burned. The good pieces I stack onto the pallet. I do this eight hours a day. They told us we must join the union and so I was in the union. What the union did for us was that if they were working us too hard, a piece of wood will mysteriously jam the conveyor belt, and the management will have to dislodge the errant pieces. This gave us a few minutes to take a breather.

Every two hours we were giving a 10-minute break, a half hour for lunch. Not knowing any better, I first took my sack lunch to the lunchroom, where everybody was eating on long tables. A couple of girls looked at me and showed curiosity because of my race – Chinese – and so I got glares from the silent rednecks who cud like cows, chewing their bologna sandwiches. So, my brother and I went outside to eat, sitting on the grass in the sun leaning against the aluminum siding of the factory. They told us that if we miss one day of work, we are de facto fired. And one day I just didn't feel like going to work and so I was de facto fired.

While the summer job lasted, I come home to our old house on Bay Avenue and I take a nap with sawdust still in my lungs. When I wake, I would read my Abstract Algebra book, a classic written by I. N. Herstein. That was the most productive time I ever had reading math, because it was pure joy to be doing something from the other extreme of mindless work as in the factory. Even today, forty-some years later, I could still give you the definition of a group, a normal subgroup, its centralizer, etc. One amusing incident when I was at the University of Oregon, when I checked out a book on Group Theory, the student library clerk said, "Oh, you are interested in Group Therapy." That will come sometime later, but let's not get ahead of our story yet.

Nameless

Nameless, these white petals,
Blossoming and falling
At side of this serpentine road.

I can make this journey fewer
Than a half a dozen years more.

But to see your delicate white petals
Litter as if worthless on the cold ground,
I, another nature's child, too am learning
To let go.

Nameless we remain.
Nameless we go on.

"Identity"

Given two "objects," if every feature and property of one is manifested also in the other, are they "identical?"

Well, there is Koon Woon 1 and there is Koon Woon 2. Koon Woon 1 speaking Chinese with a Chinese person in Chinese thinks in Chinese, while Koon Woon 2 speaking English with an English speaker thinks in English. Physically Koon Woon 1 and Koon Woon 2 are identical to the eyes. So, let's now forget about what goes on in the black box the brain, while we are not measuring brain waves etc. How much would I err if I say that Koon Woon 1 is identical to Koon Woon 2?

A simple solution is to give it a name. Koon Woon 1 = Koon Woon 2 in the sense that they are one and the same and *bicultural.*

Now let's have Koon Woon 1 = Koon Woon 2 speaks for himself.

"I came over on a jet from China Halloween night in 1960 and the jet traveled some 17 hours but when I got to Aberdeen, Washington State in the USA, it was still Halloween, 1960. I gained 17 hours because of the time zones. So, when idle people ask me if I will go back to China, I say, 'Why should I? I would lose back those 17 hours!'

"But having been indoctrinated with the Chinese culture for 12 years before I could fathom a single word of English, and subsequently forced by circumstances to adopt the American way of life as far as necessary and desirable, my identity is always a question.

"Let's back up a little bit here. When my grandmother and I left the mainland for Hong Kong she bought me a bottle of Coca Cola. Because we always boil our water in the village before we drink it, she boiled the Coke before she gave it to me. I am sure all the bacteria in the Coke were dead, but the fizz was gone too.

"That was a frivolous example. When I first attended school in the US I started out in the third grade although I was nearly 12. I was in the same classroom as two of my brothers – Lange who was held a year back because he had polio and John who was making normal progress. My younger siblings taught me how to pronounce words in the coat room Three months later they booted me to the fourth grade. I was alone there; no sibling there with me. Then a couple of months later got booted up to the fifth grade. There I had a choice – to be booted up to the sixth grade or to finish the year there. My parents said that there is no hurry. And so I stayed in the fifth grade for the rest of the year, and consequently was a year behind the normal progress all through middle and high school. In high school however, I went to night school for college courses at the local Grays Harbor College and earned enough credits to be a sophomore in college when I graduated from high school and with a higher GPA than high school to boot."

****

The red phone rings. "Hello, this is Jin."
"Jim here, Jin."
"No sense talking anymore. You got three nuclear aircraft carriers in our waters. I repeat, we are not giving an inch."
"Hey, we are not talking about your pecker. Just FON's."
"We got 1,000 DF-21d's on each one of them bastards. Don't come any closer."

There was some noise on the line. Then the phones went dead. Unbeknownst to either party, the Russians had severed the undersea cable.

It wasn't about ordering Chinese take-out in a Maryland restaurant; it was about the possible end of the world, and while people in the US believes in Heaven and Hell, so do the Chinese, except that there are more Hell's and Heaven's than you can count, they simply call it the "myriads."

My Second-Maternal-Uncle's name was Li Gar Sum, which means the myriads of the Li family. Li-Peng who had ordered the Ten An Men crackdown was a "family" member. He ordered the machine guns to be mounted against the self-same Chinese protesters and mowed down 3,000 of them. What courtesy is he going to show you, if you think that you are an 800-pound gorilla in a Chinese restaurant, sitting wherever you like?

From 1992 to 1994 when I was homeless and "sleepless" in Seattle, due to a contrived eviction from the Republic Hotel in Chinatown, I was able to receive a bi-monthly letter from my Uncle.

He scared the hell out of me because his thinking was so archaic and correct. I complained to him about my family, who ousted me when I got sick. My Uncle wrote, "He who wants offspring must obey filial piety." I was prepared to be childless, but I did not want to die, yet, and if you follow what is *unstated*, you will know that a father has a right to kill his son who does not follow the family line. But after the shock and fear wore off, I had another interpretation of what he wrote – If my father does not live up to his role of a father, he cannot have more children, one way or another. But I cannot know or decide, since I was mentally ill, or so it is thus defined by this American culture.

I separated from my Uncle at age 11. I had never responded to his letters until my father had died on Wednesday, March 26, 1986. It was my duty to then to write to Uncle and he ascended to be my Godfather. He was my protector and mentor. And only out of moral obligations am I obligated to him in any way. No one can punish me anymore, except criminal and civil laws if I violate them. Since it was told me that my father Locke Chiu Wah was the head of his village of his generation, then that role has been transferred to me. It does not matter that it is no longer practiced by the majority of Chinese in the US; the old ladies of Seattle Chinatown speak my name with some reverence.

****

It was a particularly forlorn night when I walked up the "Ave." I had sat at the Last Exit reading Oblomov until closing time at 2 AM. Then I stopped at the Coffee Corral for a cup of black coffee, before I made my way past 45th. Suddenly there appeared a fog that had enveloped University Way when I made it as far as the Continental, otherwise affectionately known as "The Greek." I heard someone called my name out of the fog. Since visibility was no more than a few feet, I could not see who it was, but it sounded like my own voice, kind of low and a bit sounding like the news commentator Daniel Shore.

"Who is it?" I said to the fog. There was no answer. I had read that if you hear your name out of the blue, it is not "hearing voices." It was around this time that I was going downhill like Oblomov, the character in the Russian novelist Goncharov's book by that name. It was around this time that I thought the checker master at the Exit was an FBI agent. More and more, people seemed to have double identities. And there was not much holding me together. I had a room in the basement on 16th and 52nd for $40 a month. My sole income was grading math papers for the UW math department, a job I held when I was a student, but I kept the job without alerting them when I had dropped out of school.

That was the third time I had dropped out of school. The first time I told Professor Isabella Yen and she said, "Someday you might come back and when you do, you will be a very good student." She was right, but she was 40 years ahead of her prognostication. She came to the Chinese class late one time, the only time she was late, and told us that some young man had broken into her house. She told him that she feels about him like a mother and it was all right to tell her what was bothering him. The young man had cried and she arranged for the mental health professionals to talk to him and gave him a bed at Harborview Hospital. But honestly, I cannot tell you if that were true, since she was teacher of Chinese literature. My Uncle in China used to tell me stories about himself but I always had a notion that literature and life are interchangeable.

Well, back to someone calling my name in the fog. I decided to ignore it. And suddenly the fog lifted. So, did I imagine the fog? Today I might call it "the mist of the world," after some Buddhist notion. I wanted to be a mathematician, but somehow my mind was drifting as if in a fog. I loved to read, because then my poverty seemed like a medal for living with minimum daily requirements.

So, I decided to push the night until morning. I went up to 52nd to the Hasty Tasty. Herbert was cooking that night. Many years later, I read he was a friend of John Nash of the "A Beautiful Mind" fame at Princeton, where they both earned Ph.D.'s. It was around that time that I carried a book by Epstein called The Theory of Gambling and Statistical Logic. Herbert took one look at it and shook his head, "I don't believe in it." Herbert was the math Guru of the underground. Dick Horn was picking his brain every night. Dick Horn went to Chicago and got a master's but still ended up flunking the prelims at the UW Math department. Herb had a protégé and his young gay lover whom we dubbed "Supertalk John," because he likes to spice up his conversation with big academic words. He dabbled in math also, and one time at the Coffee Corral he gave me a table of algebraic elements and asked me if it was a group or not. I methodically checked the axioms and found that it was not "associative." John said, "OK, wise guy, you got me this time." He was a slim little guy with those round gold framed eyeglasses like John Lennon. He told me he went to NY and said that you can either eat well, live well, or dress well in NY, but not any two or all three of those things. I told him that ever since I had read Lorca's <u>Poet in New York</u>, and the poem in it called "The Urinating Multitudes," I never had a desire to go to NY. Similarly, I never wanted to go to Europe.

Those big coliseums, imposing churches, castles, viaducts, and art work are imposing. They tend to diminish me rather than to uplift me. It is a kind of immodesty. I always felt that since life is short and gods don't exist, those monuments to the dead or the implausible are over the top. Instead, I wish I never had left my village. The history of China is what I would call "reluctance." We had to keep up because of invaders. We invented gun powder but we put it to innocuous use, not for guns but for firework. We had the best shipbuilding and sea navigation in 700 A.D. but we let the ships rot on dry dock, because we thought we were the "Middle Kingdom." That was our damning flaw. Little did we realize that not the entire world was satisfied with what they have. And Europe was practically starving when China was at its peak. So, we have been paying the price of complacency and myopia for the last 400 years of foreign domination, by people we deemed to be "barbarians."

It's all I've got, he said...

The light rain, he said, and the occasional let up's all I've got,
And walking around the block's an adventure then...
He used to write poetry, went surf fishing, my one line tossed
into the ocean, He said, is all I can do, now at night the phone
cord slips like a snake into underworld catacombs...

I used to chop at Whitman's block of wood, he said, but I
cannot gallop like Robert Frost, even walking in the woods you
would pick up some dirt, and since no woman would, himself
he caressed and said, it's all I've got...

He used to know the seasons' birds and the afterglow of the
summer sun in meadows, now he reads Anne Sexton and is no
longer concerned if the soul survives; the other day I looked
through the peephole of a construction site, he said, good
people will no longer live in houses of wood, high in the tower,
they will try to prove the existence of dirt.

In San Francisco in my torrid hour, he said, when Hamlet's
soliloquy was about me, an old poet came to see me and said,
Africa's darkest troubles are caused by diamonds, which last
forever...

He said, I'm tired of talking. Can we walk around the block?
Here are the dandelions and the weeds that push their way
through the cracks of the sidewalk, a solitary dandelion
sometimes showers in its yellow gold, its bloom many times
brighter than the sun. It's all I've got, he said...

II.   **[Many were born in this land]**

Mr. Schiller and the Genius at the Triple –
"Do you need help with going to the bathroom?" he asked.

"No," I answered. This was the first of a series of questions that I didn't feel like replying to, as it was cold and austere in his office. "Do you have any dietary restrictions?"

I didn't like the word "restrictions" and so I said "No." The snow was drifting down outside the window. I had lugged my suitcase from the road to this compound because the taxi couldn't drive in the uncovered snow. It was a bad year in Seattle. The worst snow in 20 years. But the hospital paid for the cab.

"You know," Mr. Schiller peered over his steel-rimmed glasses, "Mr. Woon, I think you are a smart man. You can think your way through troubles, and so I don't think you will be here too long."

The space heaters made a clicking sound. The heater was trying to come on, but it rather sounded like Morse or military codes. And Mr. Schiller was not a literary figure but a former colonel in the Air Force.

"Do you have a will?"

I did not answer. Such a question is not culturally-sensitive.

"Do you have a will?"

He asked again. His head had suddenly looked very large.

"I am very tired," I feigned in a weak voice. Can we do this interview at a later time? Now I do need to go to the bathroom.

"You will do just fine here. I am thinking of putting you to work here. Being part of the scheme of things will make you feel more at home here." He then "volunteered" me to help the breakfast cook to wash dishes.

"You won't be here very long," he repeated. He picked up the phone, and a few minutes later Andy came and led me to my cottage.

I saw three beds in my room, one of the three rooms in the cottage. I peered into another room where the television sound bites were coming from. I saw three motley men sitting at the edge of their beds, each watching to a separate TV. I thought, "Oh shit, here is where I am going to be, waiting for Godot."

But then I remember what the Colonel had said, "You won't be here very long."

I saw that in the alcove there was a little table with a jigsaw puzzle in progress.

I sat there for a moment. I looked out the window. I was in my winter jacket and the cottage was unheated. The snow was drifting down. It was 4 pm or so, but it was already getting dark and the white snowflakes drifts and drifts down, and some of them landed in the crotch of a birch tree.

I realized finally I was at the Triple L. I was not in a hurry to meet my fellow residents. I took out my journal. This was going to be a serious writers' retreat.

****

The cook's name was Beth. She whispered in my ear that it was really Schickogruber. She is fond of yelling at the motley crew who show up for meals. "Yak, yak, yak!," she'd yell, "you don't work, you don't eat." It struck me as being cruel because I am along with all these mentally ill and disabled people could not pull our weight out there. Who wouldn't rather have a home with a three-car garage? Expense accounts for vacation in the French Riviera. Even if one's ugly or has peculiar needs, one can pay for an escort.
Here I was at my second half-way house. The first was at Conard House in San Francisco, after my release from Napa State Hospital in Imola, California.

Who the hell do you think you are?

There isn't that much to scrutinize about my life. I am narcissistic. My father, a fry cook for the mayor's smoke shop café in a small town, scolded me, when I wanted to wear contact lenses because many high school kids were wearing contacts, "Who the hell do you think I am, and who the hell do you think you are, even President Johnson wears glasses!" But I went to the optometrist anyway and tried contacts. The optometrist put them onto my eyeballs with his fat fingers. I sat for an hour. The lenses burnt like hell and my eyes watered.

"You are too sensitive," the optometrist said. That was before soft plastic lenses. Long before "plastic" was the "one word" in the movie "The Graduate."

I remember reading Carl G. Jung's book <u>Man and His Symbols</u> in Mr. Ackerland's World History class during idle moments. Mr. Ackerland come up the isle and looked to his left at me and shook his head and smiled, "Who are you trying to impress, Woon?" But it was nearly 40 years before I really understood what a "symbol" was. A symbol is not just a word or a design, but it was a real thing! A military tank is a symbol of a soldier's penis and a nuclear bomb is a symbol of ultimate brute force. And E = mc2 is the symbol of ultimate knowledge? Mr. Know-it-all? I know Einstein did not think that way of himself. But a symbol is mistaken for the real thing or worse, we forget about the real thing behind the symbol, and there lies the danger.

"Have you ever wondered about the interior of a delusion?" My psychiatrist friend asked me. "It is like the plasma of the sun; it keeps bubbling in intense heat and metamorphosing without end!" I have delusions all my life. Let me tell you the one I had in San Francisco when I was first psychotic.

I was young Rimbaud before I wrote verse or sold my ass on Market Street. As I was walking down California Avenue to City Lunch Café on the way to work as a prep cook I walked by a telephone booth. The phone rang. A limo was parked next to the phone booth. I answered the phone and said, "No one is here to answer the phone." I walked on briskly to work.

****

Kitchen of the China Star Café.

Uncle Harry, visibly excited, pointed out to Hank and I, who were just 10 and 12 at the time, the headline on the Aberdeen Daily World newspaper: China explodes first atomic bomb. "We are catching up," he exclaimed, "we won't be the sick man of Asia forever!" My father was less sanguine, he did not say anything about that, but he told Hank and me to peel a sack of onions in the storeroom. This is what I did not like. Hank is faster than I am and he liked to make a race out of it. I feel anger and humiliation to be beaten by my younger brother.

At home we overhear our father say to our mom about his cousin, Uncle Harry. "Bail him out of jail again. Always drink until he is puke on the street."

"You can't blame him. He got no family here. He go back to hotel room and look at the four walls like a crazy man."

"He accuses us taking all the profit. Your children are white and fat, He say."

"He don't mean it. Maybe he is envious. But you got kids soon grow up to help you."

My father was mollified. My mom goes back to sewing a shirt from scratch. She had worked as a seamstress for my aunt Gim Gee in San Francisco. Immigrants like to sew up three industries – food, clothing, and housing. These are things everyone needs everyday. Not even sex is needed so often. But once you got the basics down, you can entice people to the vices and launder money into the restaurants, sweatshops, and real estate. Chinese are big on gambling.

****

Somewhere near the pasture town of El Vira, Oregon, the Greyhound bus veered off the two-lane country road, crashed through the wooden fence, careened on two wheels before it landed on its side. The driver had suffered a heart attack. The twenty or so passengers crawled out of the bus slowly, not taking any of the overhead luggage with them. I was the last one to get out of the bus, because I had wakened from a deep-stupor. I had just finished my finals week as an undergraduate student in mathematics and I had a huge sleep-debt. It took me a while to orient myself. Everyone seemed to suddenly disappear as if through a wormhole in space. I started walking in a daze and gradually I recovered my sense of self, but the grassy pasture gave way to soggier and soggier footing, and finally after about 100 or so feet, it turned into a field of rice paddies. I was walking in water-covered mud. I was incredulous. This can't be reality. But somewhere in my loyalties it was, and I had John Wisdom for a professor of "other minds."

Autumn half over

This is where I begin again, knowing the wistful air, my
shortened breath. I flit a bit more as an errant bird.
Perchance we will hold hands now and walk that far, when
snow falls, on my sparse hair. And you will finally
appreciate crows, what they know. I don't know that much
of the seasons. Except that there are four.

We have faced the rumbling of oblivion, the erasure's call.
No one can teach us now. We must hope that along with
mistakes, a bit of luck would fall.

Fifty years ago, we lived in a tenement in that lovely city
and received letters from our friends in a Turkish prison,
doing time mainly for youthful follies. The trains do not run
at midnight in that country. Letters stopped coming.
Meanwhile we drank espresso in North Beach. And I scored
Galois cigarettes. It is a spelling error. I do not know French.
Nor would I ever go to Paris and sit at a sidewalk café and
tune my poetry as I would a guitar.

A village boy from China, I boated half-way around the
world. School opened up libraries for me. I am one story
among the many my father was too busy to tell. He had been
the captain of the San Francisco Chinatown volleyball team.
My older cousin Benson told us when visiting our town
Aberdeen, and before returning to San Francisco, he gave his
BB gun to my brother Hank. Then Benson joined the Air
Force and learned to shoot an automatic rifle. Then, America
was relatively at peace, he pulled weeds at Golden Gate
Park; he was a gardener for the City. He was the oldest of
eight siblings and soon enough they all had children. My
aunt was their mother and she operated two sweat shops
that employed a total of 80 illiterate women that are
inarticulate money machines. She wanted to open a third.

License was denied. Benson went to a hearing in the city council, and he shouted these very words: "Jesus Christ, we are just trying to make a living!"
We lived in the Stockton where Crazy Annie shouted at people from her second-floor window. My friends were on welfare and their tenement room was a depot in the Hippie underground railroad that somehow always managed to have drugs of some kind. A friend of theirs was convinced he can fly off the Golden Gate Bridge and go directly to Heaven like Icarus. He went down into the water instead and was so relaxed when he hit the Bay water only his legs broke, thus dubiously becoming the first jumper to survive the Golden Gate. That's because he had already given all his worldly possessions away. Saint Peter will not take you if you are a welfare case in Heaven.

Taking it as it comes

Can't afford anything this night but the streets, walking by Foster's I see a man prone and motionless on the sidewalk. I go next door to alert the hotel clerk that possibly someone is dead. He hurries out. Upon shaking the man by his ankles, the clerk has this to say, "Don't worry about him; he is just in a drunken stupor." I then keep on walking on Market Street. San Francisco at night is neon. I still have not claimed my baggage at the Greyhound Depot. I need to find Fred and Alex. They are a gay couple I knew in Seattle. But now it is three in the morning. I impulsively come down to San Francisco, and although I have relatives here, I don't feel like I can meet them like this. I need to walk some more hours until it is dawn in North Beach. I have only a twenty bill in my wallet, a choice between breaking it on a pack of Marlboro or a cup of coffee and a donut at Foster's. I could not make decisions like these and that is the reason they reject me from the Army. Sally says that I have to measure a sandwich with a ruler before I cut it in half.

She thought

She thought maybe she could love me
But she was caught between comfort and chaos

She thought she could have it and eat it
In both ways she could affirm and also assimilate

But the upshot was not what it seemed to be
The invisible constraints keep one in place

She couldn't decide to be Alice or to be the Queen

But no matter, the importance of it all unraveled at the
seams.

Early Years in Aberdeen

The time my father arrived in Aberdeen was 1951. He didn't want his sons grow up to be gang members in SF Chinatown. He had been one and decided he rather chase the American dream in a small town on the West Coast. Hank, his first son in America was born in a taxi on the way to the hospital. That's why Hank was always in a hurry all his life. My father worked for his Uncle Benny at the Canton Café. My dad was the strongest and so he had to stay after closing time to clean the stoves and the grill, while the other cooks were taking a shower. Benny otherwise overworked my dad and my dad had one kid after another for several years. Though my dad complained about his low wages, Benny would say to others, "He's got so many kids hanging onto him like grapes on a vine, where is he going to go?" And so one Christmas they had a dinner party at the café and my dad had to cook all the steaks. Benny picked out the smallest one and gave it to my dad. My father handed it over to the waitress and walked out into the night.

He then worked at Ocean Shores Inn and later at the Smoke Shop Café owned by the Aberdeen Mayor Walt Failor. That's when I arrived from China in 1960. We lived in the Aberdeen housing projects. Then there were 9 of us in a small three-bedroom duplex. Then my dad worked for Sally in Montesano. She was the madam of a whorehouse. I helped my dad with kitchen work at the China Doll Café, the cover for the house of ill repute. The real business was upstairs. I was confused at age 14, and got more confused when the cops started coming in because the girls were in trouble. When the madam was run out of town, she stayed with us at our housing project on Oak Street for a week or two until she came up with the money to pay the sheriff in order to leave town. She claimed to be giving work to troubled girls who could not otherwise find work. And she gave me a tape recorder that was hardly used. Years later I figured out that she was taping and blackmailing her "johns." It was OK to run a clean house of prostitution if she paid off the mayor and the sheriff. But it was not OK to blackmail people. She was always telling me to ask the old lonely men to give me quarters for the juke box on slow Sundays. She told me her favorite fruit was blueberries. I went out to the foothills of the Olympics to pick a pint of it for her and I put it in the walk-in fridge for her. She never ate a single one.

Sally was always saying it is too cold in here or it is too hot in here. My dad tells me she is on too much drugs. After Sally left town, somehow my father got all the restaurant equipment and managed to transport them 10 miles to Aberdeen and started his own little Hong Kong Café right there on Simpson Avenue. He put his sons to work and when we made a go of it, his Uncle Benny finally came to visit us, and my parents cannot show ingratitude and they were solicitous to Benny about his health. I knew what to do though. I brought Benny his cup of obligatory tea. I asked, "Does grandfather Benny need some sugar in his tea?" I knew full well he had diabetes though.

How I come to be influenced by Donald Justice?

I believe I first read Donald Justice in an anthology. The poem was "Here in Katmandu." I didn't realize it was a sestina though I did detect some kind of regularity with the end words. Then I was studying mathematics and the end words were permuted from stanza to stanza. But once you choose the 6 end words, the poem can only go so many ways. I have not successfully written a sestina yet.

But it doesn't matter for I am not Donald Justice, because if you want Justice you can read him but I was not imitating him. I was influenced by him by his legal signature.

He believes in forms but I was never good at forms. Because the teacher I studied with at the University of Washington did not believe nor required us to write formal poetry. Nelson Bentley was my professor's name. He was telling us the perilous pitfalls of writing too much in form. He related a student of his had invented a very complicated form that makes the sestina look like a couplet in complexity. Nelson Bentley asked that student what he called his new form. The student said that it was called "half Nelson." But he was not satisfied with his invention and he wanted a very strict and complex form and he worked on it for years, trying to achieve the "full Nelson" as he tentatively called this new form. But alas, the pressure and task he set on himself was too great, and he went off the deep end. The men in white jackets came to get him and he was never heard of again. So, with that kind of warning I did not try to write complex formal poetry. So, the stuff I write is a cross between the traditional poetry and the Beat poetry. My publisher at first wanted to market me as a "beat poet." But I am not. Reacting to Jack Kerouac's "On the Road," I said that just because you have a car, it doesn't mean that you can drive it at 60 miles an hour all the time. But I am thankful that Lawrence Ferlinghetti blurbed my book.

It is interesting that Donald Justice makes repeated references to Wallace Stevens.

****

Three Philosophies

China has three religions (Buddhism, Confucianism, and Taoism). I am sworn to be a protector of all three. I am a member of the Triad.

In the West, the future King pulls a sword with its blade embedded in stone, while all other who tries to do so fails. In China, a member of the Triad is told by his mother, when he is old enough to understand, but never to know the truth of falsity of which, that upon his first birthday, his fate is decided. On the first-born son's birthday, all the male elders pay their visit. The male tot is placed some distance from an array of objects, and he is encouraged to approach them. The objects would include an abacus, a comb, candy, an ink brush, a piece of clothing, a musical instrument, a book, and assorted toys. The first object that the boy picks up is to decide his future occupation.

I picked up the abacus, or in Chinese, an *hsuen pan*, meaning variously as "a calculating device," "a tray of vinegar," or "a vat of sorrow." Whereas in the West, the staff is symbol of power, in some recesses of China, the abacus denotes authority. My second maternal uncle, whose name is Li Gar Sum, taught me how to use the abacus when I was five years old. He taught me the chants that go with the calculations of flipping the beads up and down the wooden tray so as to enable the hands to do the calculations without thinking of the mathematics itself. The chants direct the movements of the fingers and one needs not think of the mathematics itself. It is like an algorithm that can be performed by anyone, regardless of one's mathematical ability or insights. And so I was a robot so to speak, operating the abacus, which is the world's first computer, which they now have proven that it is mathematically equivalent to a Turing Machine. My second maternal uncle was my tutor and what was equivalent to be a godfather in the West.

I in turn have a godson, even though I have never married. The descent of power is slightly different. When my mother's younger brother's second daughter, my first cousin, was first pregnant, a gift to me of her future child was enacted in my tenement room. She gave me a choice meal. The child later turned out to be a boy and on his fifth birthday, his auntie took him to visit me in my Seattle Housing Authority low-income apartment and I had several items to give him a choice of. I presented him a guitar, an abacus, some candy, and a toy of some kind, and he chose the abacus. Looking back, I realize that his auntie had coached him on what to pick. That kind of coincides in a way that what my mother had told me about me picking up the abacus on my first birthday could have been a fabricated story, or that the abacus had been the closest object in my way. Whatever the truth is, my personal power descents to my godson and he is to receive whatever wisdom I can give him.

Perhaps it is in Fate that my mother was to abandon me twice – once when I was two, barely finished with nursing, and later in life when I developed mental illness. Circumstances were such that I did not attend her funeral, although I knew it in time, even though I was estranged from the family at the time. Fate has it also that I was separated from my uncle at boyhood and never to see him again. But I did hear his voice and his last words to me were, "Go where your heart takes you."

I've read somewhere that Chinese society is avuncular. Uncles are very important to the nephew or niece. My oldest maternal uncle told me that in ancient China, if a nephew dies somewhere, his burial is forbidden until an uncle examines the body. My oldest maternal uncle Li Gar Yee also was under the care and tutelage of his second maternal uncle. In fact, he immigrated to Peru at age 12 to join his second maternal uncle there. We will meet him again in the story later on.

Having set the story up as an avuncular relation. We are ready to move on.

The earliest I must have been five years old when he showed me the abacus. From that time on, Grandmother allowed me to walk to Uncle Sum's village alone. Uncle Sum's wife would give me a chicken thigh whenever they slaughter a chicken. Uncle Sum would teach me how to use the abacus and taught me the chants that go with the manipulations of the beads on the abacus. The reason one chants while flicking the abacus beads is that would enable one to do rote calculations without thinking.

You know I hear all these family stories told in the middle of the night after the restaurant closes. Normally in good times before my mental illness my father, mother and I would have an after closing dinner together at 1 or 2 in the morning. We three would sit at the counter at the restaurant. But they never talk about Uncle Sum. When I was in Hong Kong at age 11 Grandmother and I got a letter from Uncle Sum that his younger son had died of drowning. Shortly after that, Uncle Sum was sent to Chek Kai Island and then there was less news of him. It was not until I was 30 before I started writing to Uncle Sum. I started sending a little bit of money to him, as much as I could afford, and later I gave up smoking so that I could send a little bit of money to him, and finally when I came into my inheritance, I was able to send enough so that he could have some extras. He never abused his privilege.

I never really figured out what Chek Kai Island is all about. It could be a nursing home for invalids or it could be a prison. One of my speculations or delusions, whatever the case may be, is that Uncle had killed the person who "drowned" his son, if indeed his son was murdered. And then this goes back to an old feud. It goes back to stuff I don't know about. I have heard from Uncle's cousin Hong of Ellensburg that during the Sino-Japanese War Uncle was a "merchant" in Hong Kong. We heard that gangsters beat him up and his face was cut and the scar still remains the day he died. The recollection I have of my Uncle Sum was his house, how quiet and orderly it was. I remember his having a feather duster.

After his injuries by gangsters, he recuperated in Canton in the flat that his relatives owned. When the Communist Liberation came, they asked him to be village mayor in China. He declined. They asked him why not. He said that being an official, he would inevitably generate ill feelings with his relatives. They asked him so what. He then said, "I don't know how long your government lasts, but my relatives last forever." And so it was in Canton in the period I was there from 1958 to 1960 that when Uncle came to visit us that when he taught me how to play chess, he said, "Never wear a tall hat!" Meaning, never be an official. This is the teaching of the Tao Te Ching – "Claim wealth and titles, and disaster will follow."

Uncle had diabetes. And he is rumored to have syphilis. Unfound rumors. He lived to be 86 with a clear mind. His right leg is amputated at the knee. I remember that I had invited a boyhood friend to visit my Uncle at our flat and he made fun of my Uncle's lameness. I stopped talking to my friend. I must have been very proud and protective of my Uncle. He read me stories and taught me how to play chess. He criticized me for being self-centered and being myopic. He explained my situation to my teachers at school on why I had troubles concentrating at school. It was because my parents were overseas and my Grandmother was lax in her discipline of me.

I don't remember the exact year I saw Uncle last and it was not later than 1960, for Grandmother and I left for Hong Kong. And now more than forty years later, Uncle contacted me again by voice and I was able to say good-bye before he died.

I am talking about my Uncle, but how does it make me a member of the Triad? Where and when was I initiated? What are my duties? What secrets am I sworn to protect? And how would anyone else know that I am a member of the Triad? What happens if I meet another member of the Triad? How would we greet each other and how would we go about our business? I don't know anyone in the Triad besides my late father who claimed to be in the Triad.

Now I remember! It was the books that I read at the Canton flat by I Am a Man of the Mountain or alternatively translated, as I am a Good Samaritan. Those books were the code books of a Triad. They were sword fighting adventure stories of wandering swordsmen. I read them under Uncle Sum's guidance.

I remember my ninth birthday party in the village. All the grown men in my extended family came and an especially good meal was prepared. Men did the cooking which was unusual because women generally do the cooking. I remember my uncles asked me to eat with them. I felt like a little man.

Jose

Here is a man who has traveled and lived on three continents, only to die alone in a desolate North American hotel room. Not that he didn't have family; families he had two of his own, one in Hong Kong and one in Peru. But his spouses only gave him illegitimate children.

My uncle Jose always leaves a trail of water and bits of vegetables when he worked in the restaurant kitchen. Similarly, he left unfinished business and traces of himself where he had traveled and lived. He walked unevenly because one of his legs was shorter than the other. Born in China, immigrated to Peru at an early age, and came to Washington State when sponsored by his sister at the age of fifty, he died alone in a hotel room meant for an overnight guest in Seattle's Chinatown. Is there something that attracted people to come to Seattle's Chinatown, a most comatose place in the entire cosmos, or is it simply bad *feng shui*?

When Jose first arrived, he and I shared the old house on Bay Avenue, across the dirt field beyond which lies the rail tracks. Freights with cargo came from Georgia on the Georgia Pacific line to the Port of Grays Harbor in Aberdeen, where in the past, lumber was shipped to Japan. In exchange of lumber to build houses in earthquake-ridden Japan, we purchased the latest in consumer electronic gadgets from there.

My mother is Jose's younger sister. When our small family-owned café in the small town of Aberdeen expanded when tourism was still good, my father needed an extra hand in the kitchen. So we sponsored Jose over from Peru. Jose claimed to have worked in big *chifas* in Peru that served over a thousand people. After some familiarity with her oldest brother, whom she has not seen since she was six in China, my mother, between dinner and bar rush, would say, "Take back your wife, Poi's mother, so that you will have someone to take care of you in old age and burn incense for you in *the after.*"

"But I didn't adopt Poi," Jose would protest, "That woman did herself," referring to his legal wife in China.

80

"It is too late to argue such matters," my mother would speak a bit louder over the cracking of the hot oil in the frying wok, "Your foreign Peru woman is a foreign devil. At least your wife in China is Chinese." To this Jose had no reply. He was over fifty with a limp and dependent on his sister's family for work and company. None of them were sympathetic to his life's choices. And Jose couldn't speak English, although fluent in Chinese and Spanish.

The night that Jose died in his room at the Republic Hotel in Chinatown, Doctor Hong signed Jose's death certificate. His Peruvian wife Carmen said that she and my uncle Jose went shopping the previous day and Jose had fallen on the escalator. That's why his body was all bruised up. My mother didn't pay for the funeral and burial and so Jose got a pauper's grave. I didn't even know which cemetery. My mother had not talked to me for some time and I found out about Jose's death from my brother Lange. Lange is the bearer of bad news, as well as good news, I suppose, because he is the bearer of all news. That was his function in the family. He had the gift of gab. The rest of us did whatever work was in front of us – chopping onion, deveining prawns, whipping gravy, or ladling soup. Lange had polio in one arm and so he waited on the customers. Since none of us got paid when we worked for our family in our teen years, Lange worked for tips. So, Lange became a "smooth talker," as our family friend Marvin the Sears and Roebuck mechanic would say.

He spins it just right is the way I saw how he operated. My sister Linda said that Lange was just "happy-go-lucky." My siblings all seem to speak a different language than I did, because I was born in China, the same as my parents. My parents referred to my siblings as "jook sing" or bamboo-natured, because they were like bamboo, hard and sturdy outside, but wildly hollow inside. So, I got the burden of being the Number-One-Son. It is just some unfair game my parents played on guys like Jose and me.

"I don't know how much professor makes, I make thirty thou," is what my father says to me. I had wanted to be a mathematician ever since I saw an inspirational film about a mathematician and how goes about doing his work. The film showed a mathematician; just a man dressed casually bending over a creek and looking intently at the flow of the water. He then draws arrows on his clipboard and scribbled some letters and numbers. He is representing the water flow by a vector field. These are a bunch of short arrows that depict the direction and force of the water flow. This way he could calculate the erosion on the creek bank over time. He makes a representation of the real world with a set of diagrams and formulas. He just needed a clipboard and a pen. I thought to myself, "Wow, that's a job I like – work alone, anywhere, see things out there and inside your head. And you don't have to be in a shop or an office. That would be the ideal job for me!" And I did well in high school. But my father had other plans for me and was out to sabotage me. At least, that's what my paranoia ideation tells me now. Today I am 62 years old and my father has been dead for 25 years, a quarter of a century. And my wife tells me that I am still talking about my father as though he was in the bedroom with us. But what my parents did tell me though, one night after the closing hour of the restaurant, they took out a jade and gold set. It was an investment. They are from the old country and never trust the value of currency and so they invested in jewelry. And the Chinese value jade the most.

My mother holds up a jade bracelet. Even I was surprised at the color composition of the jade. It appeared to be milkfish with different hues of different colors diffusing in the stone, as if an orange or blue cloud would disperse and spread in the sky. "You hold up a piece of jade to the sky," my mother said, "it is looks like clouds running in the jade, then it is good jade," she said.

"Someday when we can't see you anymore, you will have some jade too," said my dad. He was wearing a soft green sweater, as if that softened him as well. That was a benign time when I was

21 years old, back from the University of Oregon, visiting for the Christmas holiday. Later on times did not prove to be so bucolic.

During the summers that I am home from the University of Oregon in Eugene, I donned on the waiter's yellow jacket, do the side work filling the soy sauce bottles, which are dark and brooding like Nietzsche, next to the white salt shakers and the pepper, a shade in between. I would wipe the already clean table tops, make an urn of Oolong tea and a pot of Simonson's coffee, I would sit quietly at a booth and read my philosophy books. The weather out is gorgeous but I could only see Mr. Besaw's hotel across the street and occasionally, Amie, who is Taiwanese married to Besaw when he was in the US Navy stationed in Taipei. She cleaned the rooms while Besaw was a buyer for the new House of Value a few blocks away on Myrtle Street, the dividing line between Aberdeen and Hoquiam.

We are on Simpson Avenue, which is coastal highway 101 going through Aberdeen and Hoquiam and we are just 3 blocks south of Hoquiam. So, one time, a very well dressed, basketball player type of a black man stepped inside the café. My brother John was with me, at the cash register, as the stranger approached. "Hey brother," he said, "I am here to raise money for bibles for our brothers at Monroe." Monroe is a state penitentiary. He spoke clearly and to the point. "Our brothers need something to read to pass the time. Can you help?" I looked at John and he looked at me. What it looked like was that even if John and I fight the guy, we would get the worse of it, as there is no one in the café but us. Our parents had gone to Seattle for the day to buy special Chinese groceries for family use.

"I am just the manager," I said, "and I can't make money decisions like those." He took a step forward and I am glad that there was the counter between us.

"Look brother, I have obtained special permission to do this." He took out a letter written on police department stationery. He thrust it to me to read. I read it carefully and slowly. I shook my head.

"Why are you shaking your head? Our brothers need the word of God to guide them through slow, difficult times."

"I am unable to help you," I said. I looked at my brother John who was visibly nervous. The black man let out a sigh and looked at John and said, "Is he your brother? I have a letter here signed by the Chief of Police that permits us to solicit on behalf of our brothers doing time." John took a step backward. He was trained in Gungfu but 130 pounds is no match for some ex-marine-looking dude. H was easily over six feet in his stocking feet and naked on the bathroom scale registering more than 250. John quickly looked back at me, with his eyes pleading. I stood my ground, "I am unable to help you," I said again. The boss isn't here and I am unable to make decisions to give to charity.

"O man, all we are asking is $40 bucks for some bibles," he said indignantly but more negotiable.

"I am sorry, my friend. We are in business and the rule says that I cannot make decisions that I don't have the authority to," I said without any quivering in voice or varied my stance. I stood squarely in front of him separated by the coffee counter. I think he could still throw a punch at me with his long arm and the punch may connect.

He stared at me with a sense of disgust and ultimately, a sense of disappointment. He turned to leave, and when he reached the door, he said, "Our brothers in prison will be disappointed not to be able to read the word of God."

When he was gone, John asked me, "Weren't you afraid of him?"

"Business is business. No monkeying," I said. "Giving money away is not the way to do business. But you know what?"

"What?" said John.

"The guy didn't know he was in Aberdeen. The letter was signed by the Hoquiam Chief of Police. And we are over the border into Aberdeen. He didn't know the difference between Aberdeen and Hoquiam. He didn't know that Myrtle Street was the dividing line!

"Wow, I still would be afraid of him," John admitted.

The Slow Hours

In the slow hours of the café, I read books. My father would work in the kitchen and I would be out waiting on tables. My mother didn't come to work until about six in the evening, as she had the responsibility of the household with a husband, eight children and herself. My father and I would come to work about two in the afternoon. I would don on my white waiter's jacket, fill the soy sauce, black pepper, salt, sugar, and napkin holders and clean the ashtrays from the previous night. I would make tea in the urn and make a pot of fresh coffee. After those and other side work, I would sit quietly in a booth and read books.

We would only have a stray customer or two until about four thirty or five o'clock, when people start coming in to eat dinner. This was in the summer time, when there was the sunshine of honey outside and the quiet hum of the beer and wine cooler kept me company inside.

In my teenage years from sixteen onto my early twenties when I came home from college in the summers, I would get into this routine. I was waiting for the world to happen. And sadly, it never did open up for me, due to my bipolar illness in my mid-twenties. But that's a story for later. For now, it is the story of the waiter.

The first book that made me cry I remember was Charles Dickens' Oliver Twist. But I did not feel that I had any sensitivity to literature. I was more interested in reading philosophy. I read Nietzsche, John Locke, Marx, Schopenhauer, Wittgenstein, John Wisdom (who was my philosophy teacher at the University of Oregon) and a host of analytic philosophers.

Although I was appointed literary chairman in my senior year at Aberdeen high school, my father did not allow me to stay after school to participate. So, all the teenage years were just school, work, and reading whenever I could get it in. I would also read books of a practical nature. I read books on buying and selling stocks, economic history, and even Mao Tse Tung's books on literature and contradictions. My mind was bombarded with both Eastern and Western ideas, as I read the Tao Te Ching and Freud in one breath.

There was one girl who came in alone and sometimes with her sister. She usually sat alone and drank black coffee in the slow hours of the restaurant. She had these dark Spanish eyes. My parents disapproved of me flirting with girls. And like an obedient first-born son and China born besides, I was expected to someday marry a Chinese girl from Hong Kong and take over the family restaurant. I didn't even know her name. She was only about a year older than I was and she wasn't in school. Although she had been coming for two or three years since I was a sophomore in high school, she was always alone, without a boy friend. She said she lived alone although she had a mother. She said that her mother let her be on her own if she didn't get into trouble.

Now at the age of fifty-six, I still remember her and the sadness I felt that I had to think about geometry and Cartesian coordinates instead of dating a white girl. My family controlled me to the very last detail of my toilet article. And slowly I developed anxiety from the lack of relief and the need to get out as in a spaceship from a dying planet. I wrote this poem, thinking of that girl, and I sure as hell wished that she found happiness and was not a depressive:

Anxiety

I shall spend the rest of my years
climbing, in order to come down the mountain
as a white-beard.

I have closed doors –
rooms I won't go back to.
I have seen myself sitting
in the lobby of the Emerson Hotel, looking out
seeing young lasses and saying to myself,
"They would decorate my room very well."

A memory snags me –
the woman with Spanish eyes,
sitting at the same coffee counter
also drinking black coffee
and not a word was exchanged.

87

The pain of wild flowers in a city ravine.

I bought and sold. Sold and bought.
In the end, I didn't gain.
My hotel was managed once by Franz Kafka.
A room with a typewriter at one corner.

Despite false alarms, pinto beans
and bacon rinds sustain me,
as I listen to the hiss of radiator steam.
Unfortunately, the hotel only keeps
its registry for so long.
There will not be a record of me.
The earthmovers and the cranes
are now just across the street.
It fills me with anxiety,
because I have read ahead in the book,
and seen the end from the beginning.

There was the dark side too about my father and his business. He claimed to be a member of the Triad. He told me tales after the day is over at the restaurant.

3am tales from the restaurant kitchen

The background was the Sino-Japanese War in the 1930's in China. People had to do more unethical things to survive and to prosper. My father was a young man of sixteen and he was a bookkeeper to an illiterate criminal in China. That's what my father told me as we ate our closing meal together in the kitchen table. We sat on milk crates. It was 3AM. We had closed up Saturday night at 2AM and did all the cleaning up. Now it is our turn to eat, after the whole town of Aberdeen has eaten. In the simple fury of work, we neglected out needs. With all the lights turned off except the one naked bulb by the walk-in refrigerator, my father pours soy sauce over his rib steak which lies on top of a mound of white rice on a steak platter. He seldom eats vegetables. I had stir-fried myself a plate of shrimp and garden vegetables and served it with white rice. First we ate in silence for a while. Then he began."I knew a guy then. He knew business. He even brought dog meat and sold it from village to village." My father took out a Marlboro cigarette from his white shirt pocket, lit it with a match, took a puff, and continued with his story, "but the guy was illiterate and I had went to high school and so he hired me for his bookkeeper." He paused and took a couple more puffs from his cigarette and cupped his left hand and used it as an ashtray, since we didn't keep an astray on the backroom table. He then told me that one time the criminal was desperate for money and had robbed an old woman. Later he went up to her and asked her if she remembered him. She said quite stupidly, " Of course! You are the dead-bag boy who robbed me of my grocery money! I hope you rot in hell." The criminal had no recourse but to murder her since he didn't want to be caught. But, my father, as he took his final puff on the Marlboro, said, "The guy was caught and hung." He said that without any comment. It was more or less a statement about the nature of the business enterprise.

I by this time realize that my chow har or stir-fried shrimp with vegetables had grown cold from listening to his story. It was indeed the dead of the night, time for plots and assassins to go about their business. Then suddenly my father changed the subject.

"Have you ever thought of business?" He asked. "You know, we are doing pretty good now. The bank says it will give me credit for a hundred thou. You can get your grandmother to pick a nice girl for you from Hong Kong. She will carry a purse and you can put things in it. You won't be so lonely and drift. When I was your age, I wasted a lot of time too. Until I went back and got your mom over. What you say?"

Just then the freight train whistled by a few blocks away. It was close to four a.m. and almost time for sleep, after a bath at the apartment the other side of the restaurant parking lot for me. Yes, I was beginning to feel a sense of losing direction. I no longer read Nietzsche with adolescent adoration. I still couldn't understand Logical Positivism. Mathematics no longer seems to satisfy my longing. I was to waste several years drinking, betting at the racetrack, and smoking dope until I would have a psychotic break with reality. This was still a relatively benign time, but loneliness was eating me like a time bomb.

We finished eating. Our house is in the back of the restaurant. My mother usually doesn't eat at night with us and she's gone into the house to watch a late show on television or to wash her hair. I said good night to my father and walked across the parking lot of the restaurant to our apartment house where I had one of the three apartments.

I remember Uncle Harry who used to be partners with my father in Hoquiam. After closing, Uncle Harry would go to a bar and invariably drink until he passes out in the streets and then my father would have to bail him out of jail. Uncle Harry's wife was in China. And he had a sleeping room at the dusty Emerson Hotel. My brother Hank and I used to have to go and wake Uncle Harry up to come to work.

Well, my bath is ready. I will soak my tense and tired muscles. Smoke a couple of cigarettes in the tub. It was suffocating to be in Aberdeen after attending the University unsuccessfully. I was beginning to suspect that I was failing but I didn't know why or how to stop it or where to get help.

Dissatisfaction and Departures

Being one of five Chinese families who are all related and all in competition with each other operating Chinese restaurants, we did not much get along with each other. My parents did not allow me to socialize with anyone. I found solace only in the middle of the night playing chess out of a book. I was in all modesty fairly bright in academic subjects and had been in a "bright and gifted" seminar for high school students at Western Washington State College after my junior year in high school and was asked by M.I.T. to apply to them. But I really was not socially well-adjusted. I was lonely and I wanted to escape somehow the rigidity of a conservative logging and fishing town. This next poem aptly characterizes how I felt:

Aberdeen, 1966
Or, Driving Around for a Poem

Driving behind a logging truck with dancing flags
Pinned onto the logs, I listen to "Norwegian Wood" by the
Beatles
Miss Freeland wants a poem for her creative-writing class.
In the Pulse of saw mills I cut this logging town
Into board-feet with my '55 Plymouth, with sawdust
Plenty to make ice-cream cones. I tend to forget
The manure that gives us Red Delicious, or this memory.

Between windshield-wiper swings I hear the tugs' blasts.
Perch and red snapper flap on Scandinavian boats.
Neighborhoods where I sold the *Reader's Digest*
In Finnish or Polish editions. Catching a glimpse
Of a girl at the S.H. Kress coffee counter, I think
Of the book on the backseat, *Eleven Kinds of Loneliness.*
The doctors in
the antiseptic Backer Building can't take away
This and other pains of a small town.
It is near Xmas. My little brother peeks out the window
Of the car. He is promised hot dogs and ice-cream for
coming along.

If a pretty girl raises her umbrella, I'll write a long poem.
No such luck. We cross over to Cosmopolis to see
Boys fishing the Wishkah for sturgeon.
The car is damp, the heater doesn't work.
In the monotony of rain and windshield-wiper swings
I think I have a rhythm to beat the words against.
My brother and I settle for hog dogs and milk shakes
At a drive-in going out of town.

Anther poem about departures from Aberdeen is the following:

Flight

                                    **Oak Street never
had oaks: this much we knew**
                of the street we lived on. Aberdeen
In the encyclopedia refers you to Scotland.
                        You know,
Nineteen years of it is visual purple,
A shiver when you have the right answer in a high school
math class,
        A 35-pound salmon on a 20-lb. test, a 1909-S VDB penny.

The Rain Derby, to guess the year's rainfall to the nearest
                        hundredth of an inch, and
An occasional carnival keep he town buoyant,
Even though half of the graduating class leaves Aberdeen.
When they come to the Satsop River,
        A slender body of water like a nun,
Never pregnant, not even in the rainy seasons,
They hesitate, but only momentarily, before pretending to be
Alexander the Great crossing the Tiber.

Channel cats (catfish) would either dig a hole
                in the muddy bottom, lodge themselves, vacuum
All the food that drift their way, or swim downstream
forever.
        Hank keeps coming back to Aberdeen for his limit of razor
clams

     at Oyehut, to find
  His poker luck at the Spar, to his ex-wife and two kids,
  To bowl at the Harbor Lanes with Frank, the Taholah Judge,
  To the blueberry shrubs only he knows where in the foothills
of the Olympics.

The Old House

    Across dirt field,
Freights rumble through the evening pyre of burnt summer;
Light, off burnt grasses, raw honey, reflects
Into the anteroom through the blinds like X.J. Kennedy's
"Nude Descending Stairs,"
Rinds of light, yellow like bovine teeth,
like a manila envelope full of old receipts.

Also, milkfish, jade-green lights refract
Through the crabapple tree into the bedroom where I rest,
after swimming against the current for so many years in the pre-dawn
Light, no longer measuring myself against
The significant digits of the slide rule.

And the table lamp, incandescent, floods the room with yellow
Light at night on a yellow pad of paper. Here, was a birth
Of a thought which is not born is either ageless or will not live at all.

I began to trust the hand that guides a scalpel,
The hand that dress a wound.
     The old house is
a kind asylum for Soviet dissidents
Who escape by turning themselves into spiders and traveling across
the Tundra.

I lived here in Plato's Cave and dreamed of the Platonic heaven.
I studied the shadows. And Hank?
He is playing the Wednesday night Bingo.

It Comes Through the Branches

The crabapple tree, dense with leaves, wounded by age, its foliage
Fluttered open and closed.
Branches flutter, from this we know wind through gaps of leaves, like blanks
In my diary, where a subterranean form fluctuates through the years.

The forgetting function which forgets its argument, yet I remember the window pane
Where emerald light streamed in. The question may go like this of my life:
"And where were you on the day in question?"
The answer may be: "Sir, all my days are questions, but on that particular day,
I was leagues under the sea, of all things, naming, naming the things of this world:
    A name is a handle on a cup, a tag on a suitcase.
    I call Sam Sam and Harry Harry ---
    Confucius said the first step to knowledge is calling
                things by their correct names..."

The crabapples, stems, triangular leaves silhouette on the old house window pane
Like Sheffer strokes and other symbolic logic notation. The closure of the tree
Was the world. The knowing and the known once twirled in the bedroom like a
Flamenco dancer to the guitar of Carlos Montoya.:
    Naming was a game on daffodils,
    Ferns and clovers on the hills.
    We live, we name, what we love, we love is name.

In one summer, the life span of insects.
In one afternoon, the tree flutters open, the tree flutters closed.
My ears, heavy with the music now. Think: Does the Oak care if you call it "Oak?"
Does the rose care if you call it "rose?" All language is naming. Sometimes
All you have to do is mention it: Say wind through the chimes and water on the Thames.
Say water rippling against the sand bar and fingers plucking the guitar...

Aberdeen was an isolated fauna and flora like the Bushmen's song of a distance,
Like the crucible in which we burnt things in high school chemistry,
Like creatures in a tide pool at Point Grenville.
This was Aberdeen, where I changed although my name remained the same.

Madam Amara

Two detectives came. I had called them for my Fat Aunt.

My Fat Aunt is squat and her head looks like a catfish's. Her son had been shot and killed in a gang-related matter. This happened very suddenly when I was in Seattle, making a last ditch attempt to study math. My dad had called me home to Aberdeen.

Benny Locke had interviewed the guy in San Francisco, my dad told me. It was at 3 AM after the family restaurant had closed for the night. My dad and I sat on milk crates in the kitchen with only one naked bulb on. We were sitting at our make-shift table. My dad had split an Oly beer with me. He said a small amount of alcohol was good for his high-blood pressure. Benny was my dad's "uncle." He was the oldest of the Locke families in Aberdeen. My Fat Aunt was my dad's older sister who married the Lau Family in San Francisco.

I saw my Martin all aflame, said my Fat Aunt. He said I am parched and I cannot rest in peace. I said drink a cup of forgetful tea my son and you can leave Purgatory and transmigrate. But mother if I came back as a puppy at your doorsteps, how would you recognize me? Martin was all aflame. He wanted satisfaction.

Quanyin the Goddess of Mercy was sitting on a lotus and through the chains of lotus hearts she is connected to every eel and owl, steel needle and human nerve. She hears all and forgives all. She heard the anguish of my Fat Aunt and Martin her son's cry for satisfaction. In the real world Fat Aunt called her "uncle" Benny and Benny ordered my dad to call me home from Seattle. Dutifully I came back to Aberdeen.

There we were sitting on milk crates. My dad smoking a Marlboro and used his left hand cupped as an ashtray. When his cigarette burnt to the very end he held the butt straight up until it extinguished. He walked over to the restaurant kitchen sink for good measure turn the faucet on the cigarette. He rinsed his hand. Coming back to our makeshift table he spied the stove pilot lights with a quick glance. He was always afraid of fires. He had worked in a match factory in China.

"He got through by climbing the bedroom window. He approached the sleeping couple. His faithless girl and her new boyfriend of the other gang. He advanced toward them with a knife. The new boyfriend was startled and whipped out his gun under his pillow. He fired rapidly and struck Martin in the neck. Martin staggered back a step and resumed advancing. Another shot was fired and it also struck Martin in the neck. Martin staggered again but was determined and advanced again. This time the new boyfriend fired two rapid shots at Martin's neck. Four shots total to the neck. Martin finally dropped inert onto the bedroom floor."

Benny told my dad that. My dad told me that it was self-defense.

I was "urged" to go to SF to cheer my Fat Aunt up. I got on the Greyhound. I did not realize that a whole new chapter of my life would begin. At age 27, I had been a miserable failure at work, school, and romance. After this trip, I would be in colossal disarray for 3o years. So, here I come for the "adventure." Madam Amara will be an inconsequential character in this narrative. She will be arrested as she is a minor con artist. The two SF detectives told me that con artists are usually nonthreatening. They had her arrested shortly after I interpreted for my Fat Aunt how she con my aunt money in her grief.

Often a man

Often a man listens to faraway woods, like a wolf may pause
In snowy shadows for winds that may bring the aroma of
bread,
And reflects on the glory and the shame of the pack,
How it hunts and tears flesh from flesh, sips blood from the
jugular of
A lamb, and how yet when the pack moves stealthily by a
country church
In the moonlight that falls and glides on the frozen fields
To the ailing schoolhouse, their bags unzipping to penciled
wisdom
Gleaned between the milking of the cow and blowing out the
long candle
In the childhood bedrooms that fill all farmhouses that flock
together
For comfort and company, and in their communal pledges,
Erect churches where the pastor says it as best he can.

The man often hears blood in this ears when in his bed alone.
He looks up at the ceiling and he knows he should not be
smoking...
The woman, not his, is meticulous and tender, who at this hour
is anointing her face.
Which is already beautiful, her curls dangling at her temples,
The skin smoother than the skin of grapes, in soft whispers she
calls
The name of the man she loves but they have never met...
He is a singer who moves across the stages of the world,
More famous than Russian poets or political leaders,
He croons just three words and young girls swoon; he lines his
guitar case
With drugs and contraband goods, exits with the brutal custody
of bobbies,
And the woman, no longer a young girl, knows everything
about the singer,

And in the late hour, when snow threatens to fall on farmhouses,
She flicks on the bed lamp and reads the magazine of famous people,
Forgetting altogether the dreary hours at the checkout stand of the large variety store
Where she's a cashier, pennies go with pennies, and five dollar bills with five dollar bills.
All the while the man who often hears blood throb in his ears
Dreams about five numbers straight across, a pack of Old Gold cigarettes,
And is wondering about the feasibility of a hamburger at Jack-In-The-Box
At this hour...

A wolf too may listen to a man when a man is happy and is strumming a guitar
Like the water of six rivers, the wolf too may sing as a beast can.
After he steals the oil of sanctuary lamps and forgets about childhood shame,
He wanders over sweet grasses and white barley, his nostrils moist
And filled with the aroma of bread that rises from the chimneys of farmhouses
In little villages, out of which little boys and girls walk
Into hospitals and company-owned gift shops, or go as high as the lectern
Of a state-run university, while the man with the blood throbbing in his ear,
The woman reading the magazine in bed have never met except, unknown to each
He hands her a dollar for a lottery ticket, and she's very happy
At that precise moment because, over the music system of the store,
They are playing a song of the singer she loves...

This modal logical moment...
The guitar, its notes falling as a fountain in Spain
Modeled in tape, and bearing the agitated humming
from the typewriter...
Know: life is not forever...
As the wind and water softly whisper a record on
the beach sand
to say my life was not among the favored,
and the enormous numbers I bet on with a slide
rule
Also did not come to at the rail...
And now you are afraid of my anger, because I rip
the calendar off,
For over a half of my life I did not search in the
right places for you,
Though you saw me all the time as a hapless
Bohemian
who sees one tree and asks, "Where are the other
nine?"
And goes into a forest as one tree and becomes
lost...
And now I type into the typewriter this:
The four corners are illuminated, and this room is a
great philosophical inquiry,
Catch the light in a rented home.
We have our allotment of bugs and mice,
And in a coin-operated universe such as this one,
It is possible to punch the wrong item,
And there could be some faulty wiring,
And you may not get what you want, if you get
anything at all.
But be my friend for this evening;
I am lonely and time spreads itself languidly on the
bed,
A rented room somewhere but not far from the
tracks,
And you briefly come into it, and Unknown

stealthily seeps in,
Pretending to be wind...
I need your presence in this room; it is a good
room;
And I am doing good in this room, as Lucifer in
his way hangs onto
His corner of Hell, and all the events in the
Universe are chained,
And this is a possible room you may have passed
through,and it could also be
A necessary room for you to stay, and it is not
necessary and not possible that
It is perfect. No, it is a lit room, and a typewriter is
at one corner...

At the end of the day

When sunshine tapers off and the fiery
evening is without borders; details
having been worked out, infinite sadness
descends on the sum total of his life,
where he was a shadow at the world's
bluest place, where trees crowd
together like criminals in a penal colony,
where the closing down is anticlimactic
and eulogies are without recording.

And so it comes to this -- the morning colliding
like successive rail cars into the night;
though the shadow lengthens, its tenuous
grasp grows more and more insubstantial, until
it finally vanishes into the sand.
I am also filled with infinite sadness,
I do not regret what has been,
for it was a moment in which soy and sugar cane
sprouted, and an interval during which
men and women casually entered
and left their houses.

Not the first Encounter

I saw arrangements of chrysanthemums wet with rain
water, plum foliage hiding birds, and the tiniest
sparrows on power lines, so I wonder

How will death come when my pained body
struggles no more to allow my spirit
fly to the Cosmos,

As I meditate on these raucous black birds –
why do they not wanted to share space with me?

I have seen tiny hairless sparrows on the sidewalk dead
because of an errant cat, and don't know why this one word
triggers the ancient master Li Po as an *errant* knight
traversing the expanse of China;

If I were only part him and my verse dances from ear to
ear of my skull, sending a shiver, as

The bumble bee flits from flower to flower in
self-absorbed work, honey being its final outcome.
This meaning a sweet ending?

My knees pop from a lifetime of walking, but how else can I
contemplate the void, when death will barb me
into a circus with clowns in three rings for diversion?

Hanging onto the last minutes,
as clocks wind down with entropy,
and activities in every town that I have
been unwinding, allowing the Cosmos to sweep me aside.

I think every comment that I can make borders
on the superfluous.

Surf-fishing at Ocean Shores

With weather like the hexagonal nut I use for
Sinker, I wait for a single, clear pulse from the ocean.

I had driven past a row of townhouses which the
Crabgrass attempted to burglarize. Once there was talk
Of a casino, and a hastily-constructed golf-course had left
Celebrities standing in mud puddles.

The one existing restaurant scalps better than Indians,
Whose clam beds now lie under the molasses of an oil spill.

In the summer, a mother and a daughter painted
The surf with gentle dabs of blue and white. They painted a
boat
That wasn't there. Now it is November, in hip boots. And I
see
No charters.

What is one line in the ocean? Even as I pin a bright orange
Sand shrimp on a number-two hook. The weather is
Wrong, the mood is wrong.

I am really thinking about the Indo-Chinese refugees
Off the Canadian coast.

This town, when I come back to it, I find
Less land, more water, fewer people, fewer memories,
though

The road to it hasn't change much. The dip outside of
Hoquiam
Still makes my stomach flutter going the legal limit of fifty.
The farm house wherein lived Ron and Yushuko still

Stands, although they had moved and she later committed suicide
When he took on a young mistress. A war bride, Yoshuko
Was still obedient to her original culture.

I am drinking coffee, just coffee, from the thermo.

The sea is one heavy volume. No memory can wash one with the
Force of the sea.

M

One of M's earliest memories is her father loading every head, trunk, limb of every one of his children into his station wagon and driving to Northern State Hospital. Why, M? To see mom play volleyball.

M's daddy had a shake mill, but he drank so much it burnt down. He died of asphyxiation in bed. After that, M was in a couple of foster homes.

M completed her high school in Farfax Hospital by correspondence and she was able to receive her diploma in person because the doctor gave her a pass.

Now F is seventeen with a corn-dew sweetness and gentle soul. She broke down again because she alerted her grandmother by phone telling her not to drive because there are too many Communists on the road. In Farfax again and his time because she tries to exorcise the devils in her head by swallowing all her mom's sleeping pills. M, you silly girl. When M left the hospital, she had turned eighteen and was placed in a halfway house.

There she met K. M thought that K was really smart because K wore white shirts. Smart of not, K was nice to M. Soon she let him fondle her breasts. They became friends.

M doesn't like bees. She would gasp and scream. K would kill the bee for her. Though she loved flowers and most flora and fauna, she doesn't apologize for the extermination of bees and spiders. The thought of it, ferocious but tiny creatures offending M! K has no qualms about the killing. Neither of them was enlightened at this point.

M's mother H took M's rent money once, wrote a few bum checks, bought a car, and toured the country with her boyfriend who was M's cousin. M told K, "Mom can manipulate the ass off ya." But M still loved H. H started a couple of gardens with the belief that food will be in shortage this winter.

M and K lived with two other housemates who were all one time at the halfway house. Because of personality conflicts, all of K's other housemates asked K to leave. M didn't know whether to continue with K or not. She joined with the others but later wanted to tell him she was sorry. K moved out. M had a breakdown.

K had been bundling newspapers for an older couple who had a motorized paper route. That was the only money he could make besides his disability income. The older couple allowed him to rent a room from them. The best thing they did was also to lend him the use of their electric typewriter.

Eventually M went away and came back to see K at the older couple's house. She wanted to marry him. The older lady told K that he would be jumping from the frying pan into the fire. K had missed M. M was sweet and kind beneath it all, and though K did not seriously entertain marrying M, he wanted to remember her as someone who had share with him the best moments out of the muck they found themselves in life. K is now in a little room at the University District. He is trying to summon up love. Life is sometimes in the "as is" condition. M by then had been a memory.

But life is never going to stop until death for anyone. It could get better or it could get worse. So, it didn't stop for either M or K. In time, M will be less indecisive and maybe she can get better sleep. K is treating this like any other misfortune. It was years later he recalled the song by the Doors, "Into this world we are thrown." He has by now become a survivor. M is still young and not as well seasoned. She needs a helping hand and K is willing to provide that of course. But like Lorca in his "Somnambular Ballad," where the older man is saying to his younger compatriots, "If I were able, this bargain would be closed, but I am no longer I, nor my house is any longer my house."

****

M knows about shopping and garage sales. K knows his share of science and mathematics. An unlikely couple they were. They enjoyed each other's company because there is a deep loneliness that inhabits them. K didn't talk much, keeping his beliefs mostly to himself. But he was glad to share knowledge. Sometimes M doesn't think K loves her because he doesn't talk much to her. But K takes time to teach M things such as percentages, how it works, and what a 15% discount means and all that. M thought that K was smart and she believed that he loved her. He did, without saying it much.

Being young, M was easily influenced by other people. Her sister grew pot and shoplifted. M shoplifted and was caught. She had to pay restitution.

M liked K to sleep in the same bed with her. They each occupied a room in this communal arrangement. Sleeping together makes her feel close to someone. She was full of love. K of course would get aroused and they would make love. So, they would deprive themselves of an hour of sleep but sleeping much more soundly.

****

M's daddy had played the guitar. He had nice guitars. And he made up songs. He said he was sending the songs in. Had some sent in, etc. Had heard his own songs on the radio that someone else had recorded etc. But no one believed him because he was drinking heavily. Like previously stated, he died of asphyxiation.

K sometimes played the guitar too. And that reminded of her daddy, especially when he played, "Because you are mine." But K never thought of himself as a singer or guitarist.

****

M and K went walking. It was in the evening. M stopped K many times to point out the sunset. K was looking at the ground as he walked. M saw the beautiful sunset and she was part of this world. They walked for a long time and M felt close to K. They walked near the water and M wondered about the tides and the seaweed. For K, walking with M was better than not walking with M. And it is better to have M than not to have M. Such a mercenary mathematical attitude. So they got along in a fragile kind of bond.

****

Then it happened. M found a job at a telephone answering service. K got up very early to cook M breakfast. K thought that it would worked out as M had a very sweet voice. M found the job too hectic. She quit before the training period was over.

M was sure that K could get a job. But he never tried except getting a job at the 7-Eleven as a clerk. K's friends said that he has more guts than they do. K thought nothing of the robberies and shootings of 7-Eleven clerks. He was too dumb to realize. He was oblivious to many of the hidden meanings of the conversations at the mental health center, where they both were obligated to go.

****

M loves to bathe. K idly penned this:

> M got up and bathed
> And left a trail of
>
> Baby powder on the floor
>
> M got up and bathed
> And left a sweet
>
> Scent in her hair.

Once they went on a ferry. They sat near the window. Gulls flew by, close enough that you can see the colors in their beaks before they veer off. M said, "They are our escorts." She always said that there is one job that K could get, because of his cute butt. That was to be an escort.

****

A nameless oppression slowly overtook M. Nothing was going right. She wanted to be a flight attendant but even waitress jobs are hectic even when not glamorous. She didn't want K anymore.

At the mental health center one of the counselors cornered K and said that things wouldn't work out with M. K asked why not. The counselor said that was therapist-client confidentiality and thus it cannot be revealed. K was too dumb to complain, because telling him that it could be false or true but he can't know the reason, the counselor is clearly trying to influence their relationship. But M was finding K to be boring. He wouldn't smoke grass with her and some of the other people during the lunch break.

M said, "This is real. I don't want any of this," meaning to continue with their relationship. K was hit right between the eyes so to speak. Years later, another patient told K that one of the counselors was fucking every one of the women in therapy.

Not long after this, M had another breakdown. Not so mysterious to K anymore because he found that people in group therapy were drinking Southern Comfort in the Coke bottle. K had to move on with his life.

There was a guy we will call Alan. He had been in prison and he borrows money from K. He always paid K back before he borrowed again. He was constantly smoking weed. He said that it calmed him down because he always felt like smashing people on the head. He was court ordered to be in therapy. Anyway, they were walking to K's bank and a car came from the alley without paying attention and almost hit K. Alan jumped on the hood of the car and banged on it.

They got along. People began to know that K was once held without bail. But instead of going to prison, he was incarcerated in a state hospital in California. They also learned that he had jumped eight psych techs who were trying to give him medicine. They also knew that K was smart and was always elected president of the ward. K won't make anyone's life any worse.

But what would make K the happiest is by a fluke his mind cooperates and he could do math and philosophy again. He didn't want any of this genetic time-bomb. But here he is, on a good day his brain would stop jumping and there was no "funny business" as Dr. F uses the lingo. On a bad day K wouldn't even disbelieve that he had been poisoned by his siblings to get all of the inheritance. They were afraid of him, and that's evidence itself.

****

The year that M was away, K was trying to write decent poetry. He even took a creative writing class. But since he was lonely he wrote about loneliness. He wonders if the bird outside his window had been outside of M's window. He wrote about warriors that were crippled by a "sparrow-less night." He wrote about a ship with a broken mast and the sailors never siring children. Sometimes he would send them to M. Sometimes she replies, "Don't write unhappy stuff."

The year that she was back he entered into a literary contest at some kind of literary center by the market. What gratified K was the M came two Sundays to hear him read. Winning the $100 prize would give them quite a celebration. K's turn to read came on the second Sunday. It was a chilly day and the wind blew. They didn't have lunch money. K dredged all his pockets and found enough for a candy bar for M. M let him take a bite. They walked around the block while the judges recessed to decide. M said several times that K will surely win something. A friend that came with them said the same thing. K said that they would all eat dinner if he wins. Meanwhile the judges came out of the tavern where they had a beer to make this difficult decision. K was not on the list.

****

The Car Man

"The Lord says we got to love our enemies," said the Car Man at the mental health center. Angusto and I think though that the doctor murdered him because he complained too much how the facilities degraded over time and he depended on the place for his lunch and weak coffee. He often signaled us to walk ahead when we went to Ed's to play Spades. "He is so fat, his heart is bad, and they didn't give him a diuretic" Angusto is the guy who called up all the morgues to find and claim Car Man's 350 pound dead body to have it cremated. I was the only guy at the mental health center who didn't show up for the memorial because I am Chinese and it is my heritage that I got to stay alive if I think my friend was murdered, for I must save myself to someday revenge for him. Nobody knew that was the reason. They thought I was just sick that day. But the littler they know the better it is this way.

Car Man is Black but he wrote short stories against Jews. What do you expect from a mental patient? Half of my psychiatrists been Jewish and they are the better ones. Anna the nurse told me, "Chin, when you are fifty, that's when your friends start dying off." I was fifty. And my father told me that was the age a man was responsible for his face. He is from the old country and his English is not good. He meant that a man is responsible for his fate at fifty. I wrote a poem that I lean back from life when I became fifty and I knew I couldn't do it alone anymore. A young publisher in New Jersey published it in his rag mag, but someone liked it and it was a publication.

The Car Man was afraid to tell me where he lived though I see the Car Man five days a week, and I volunteered to cook the lunches, and Car Man and I hung out of the back door and smoked. He was not given a seat in the main lunchroom but I was. At first I didn't have a seat either, until some "leader" found out I had been a math major and he was taken electronics for computer circuitry to get back to work. He was the paranoid type. People said he spent five years under a bridge. He was a Republican. Ed was a Democrat and was into mental health issues. They were good friends and both used politics to get out of work. The leader guy helped me to do side work for the lunch I cooked one day. I spent five minutes showing him how to slice a mushroom. "First you lay it so its stem is up; you chop it in half right down the middle of the stem. And then you turn one-half so that it is flat on the cutting board, and then you slice it with chopping motions." The leader did exactly one mushroom, and then quit. He went to sit down and to drink his coffee and resumed his political talks and looked important again. I was the Chinese coolie. I didn't mind it. The bible said, "Seek ye the truth and the truth shall set ye free."

The nurse asked me what I am going to do with all of Car Man's short stories. I said I was going to publish them someday. She then told me that her teen son had died mysteriously and the Car Man was the only patient who came to the funeral. She told me that the Car Man was crossing the street from his family's barbecue eatery when he was hit by a car. It broke a couple of discs in his back. They were trying to kill him. He was lucky though there was not a real investigation. That's how he got the name Car Man.

After 45 years beginning college. I got my BA degree in BS. The medicines have gotten better. But I hope people's attitude get better as well, at least as it relates to mental illness.

My Room Squats Modestly

Not a father and no longer a son,
Soon I will enter my room at 40,
Having to accept who sits
At its only chair as a friend.
Living in a room, meant for an
overnight guest,
Where time leaks through the faucet, my pounding
On the typewriter proclaims
As well as the solitary insect rattling
Its antennas on the dresser.
Kafka might have managed the hotel once or twice.

Late at night, the wind rolls
Empty beer cans on the roof top below, like Tibetan prayer-
wheels.
Before oatmeal, the metronome
In the grooves of my brain swings from hope to despair.
I rise and serve my room's
prisoner
Coffee and mete him a sentence life has given me.
And he is in, casts the I-Ching
And indulges nonsense like a buffoon.

That's how it is
For us who live in hotels, he says to me,
And the hotel keeps the registers
For only so long. But there is one window,
And you can look out of it,
Like the eye of Cyclops on the world.

The Usher's Tie

Our unpleasantness seated on the warm
                              colors of the sofas.
Important and appropriate the usher had a tie.
You remember the Evergreen black berries
                              we pick for mama's jam, Hank,
On the side of the railroad track? Some were
                              so ripe they didn't wait for us.
Hank was thinking three kings don't beat a flush.

Two brothers held up mama's column of grief.
The rites later will be one in Christian
                              and one in Chinese, to burn
A hell of a lot of Hell Bank Notes, a choice of heavens.

And a stone three times the size of his grandfather's.
When the rain stops in Spring when the cemetery will be firm.
The same one as Bruce Lee.

Here on I can only talk to his ghost.
The same story: railroad, restaurant and laundry
Immigrants who thought of returning but never did.
There is so much beef and duck fat.

He stood for half of his life in front of a wok
While Sonny Listen lasted three rounds
                              with who was Cassius Clay then
On the kitchen radio.
                              He is not thinking of chop suey
But his jooksing children another invention of America.

He cast his vote - almost for a democrat.
And in his village in China, the red, ripe berries
Would fall. And one did yesterday.

Under the Oak

For the woman with her diary frozen
        in the freezer like a Swiss account,
a gorged, brutal breath driven
        to shadows under the oak
        because of a cautious porch light,
is a man breaking into children pretzels.

It is beside the point she's somnambular,
        like a green woman from a green
ballustrade,
        like a stiffly moving pigeon,
        tripping out at 3 A.M., flirting, as:
Under a bridge of man's hard concrete and steel:
    A sudden glint of chrome,
    A Kamakazie plane ripping a ship,
    The scent of sacrifice,
    The enlarged breath of violence.

She had said:
    If you take, I will respond like a mummy
        with Pharoahs' curses.
    The Sixties are flowers trampled.
    And what could you take that hasn't the odor
        of a 3-day-old fish?

She unlocks the door to the house of her bodices.
She unlocks the freezer. Her diary,
gaps where she withdrew from life, feeling unsafe,
        like a flower before wanton
hands.
Only in the sanctuary of her very own bed room,
        does she feel safe from
uncontrolled
        appetites.

The Drift

"The more education you got," my father heaved one of those leaden sighs, as he wrung out the last bar towel with his old but still capable hands, "the less you see your parents as your own people." This only reinforced my plans for escape. After all, he said that our restaurant is not real business, it is just "family business," and he is always telling my mother and me how we could not function in a city. Still, I want to escape to Seattle, the first place when my plane landed eight years ago. Maybe I would find more in my father to like hadn't he been so mercilessly ambitious.

"I used to think that I can be President, but now I guess it takes at least three generations." That's the closest he admitted in pushing us to perform in school. In the national math test I scored 40 out of 80 and Tom had 60 something. We always knew his IQ was above genius level, but my humble 40 grade was second. And on that basis we went to night school together to take Calculus.

Ten years later I was living in a crack house in Seattle. It was the only place I could afford an efficiency room or apartment however you want to call it. Bathroom was still down the hall. I was also assistant manager to the holding company that bought it to sell; we were just waiting to go to a rooming house or the cold streets. And so I tried to have fewer reasons why they would need to renovate or to have it torn down. It turned out this restaurant owner on the "Ave" had bought it and one of my university friends was doing repair work on the house. I see why now after thirty more odd years that I have lived and still living. Buck told me, while he was digging the ditch, had he been female and black, he would have his own laboratory. But as a middle-class boy growing up, he didn't want to do crime. It would be easy enough for him to make money. He was a Ph.D. chemist.

I brought a cup of coffee out to Buck. He was digging a long ditch for the natural gas pipe. The new owner gave us a line of bullshit how nice the place was going to look, as soon as the renovations are done. But that bastard just want to sink a few bucks in it so that he could sell it for more, or he could hang onto it longer and the longer he waits the more money he will get for it. He was a Greek businessman. Once he had two girls walking down the street with him and he had a finger in each of the belt loops of the girls. He whispered to me, "Hey, I have two Chinese girls working for me." Little did he know, he signed his death warrant then and there.

Bookseller at Shamin

Even though paper was invented in China, paper was not cheap. And since books needed printing, there is the cost of ink. And so books were relatively expensive even though writers get only a pittance. Lordy lord, isn't this the way it always works. What stands between the writer and you the reader is a slough of middlemen. These guys are known as agents, editors, publishers, printers, distributors, and finally the bookstore owner. It is sort like a food chain, isn't it? And the writer is the bottom feeder, and that's why they write so much of the "river-bottom." Even Dostoyevsky had to take a gamble when he wrote a book. But that *lucky* guy, he got the book, the money, and the woman when he wrote *The Gambler.* I doubt it if I ever get that lucky.But when I was a kid in Canton, China, I became a book renter. You guys now just started writing comic books, after seeing the Japanese get so successful at it.. Go to the Kinokuniya Bookstore in Seattle (that's inside the Japanese shopping mall the Uwajimaya), you will find that half of the titles are comic books. However, like many things, including silk, spaghetti, and in this case, comic books, they originated in China. You didn't need to buy books to read. There are street bookstands that you can rent a book to read for a nickel or a dime. These books were not frivolous. Since many people in 1955 in China were still illiterate, and since (the Chinese say) a picture is worth a thousand words, young and old alike rented these books and hovered around the street "library." That was where most of my allowance went. And when I had enough money, let's say from New Year's lucky money that is wrapped in a red envelope, I was able to buy a particularly longed-for war book. While kids in the US read about Superman and all that fanciful stuff, we read the *real* stuff. And it makes sense that all the books I owned were war books. You may ask why don't you go to the library to read, instead of spending money to read at a bookstand on the street? Well, that is because all the books in the public library were Party literature. I don't mean books about drinking, dancing, and wild sex, I mean they were books written by and for the good of the Communist Party. Well, I will come back to this a bit later.

I had decided to be a "lending library" and let other kids read my books for a fee. So I became a pay-as-you-read book renter. I was advanced for my age. Some of the books I had were of course thicker than others. And so I take out the binding and split it into two or three sections and sewed it up. And so I could count it as two or three books, etc. It was not that difficult an idea. Once you become a merchant, you try to gouge people. Had I not have grown up and move onto other things (like sex, drugs, and rock'n roll) I might have owned a conglomerate of book-renting companies.

De la Mancha

Paper was invented when a tree fell into a pond
Ink was invented when a berry dropped onto the
ground

Don Quixote was born when Miguel Cervantes picked
up the pen
But for four hundred years we still not learned a thing

What we invent that don't kill we still have not utility
We double-down on the lethality of monstrous cruelty

The practical thing to do is still to endlessly augment
our wealth
Never mind the environmental damage to our health

When the drones come out from the local police
departments
We must stay home and read about the knightly news

Don Quixote and Sancho Panza the pair de la Mancha
We count on you!

The Little River

There is a little river sloshing in
a tenement room, bent on
getting out into the hall.

The same river they say that
began in racine hills and
will flow again with the necessary silt.

And so in this metropolis,
you find that man who is not against
pigeons, and lo and behold, the
pigeons aren't against him.

There is also a man who
philosophize at the town square and
write letters for those visually impaired.

High up in the hills the wolves
howl, with the best of them to
dine on goats' meat tonight.

Meanwhile this little river circuitously
snake about the town while the Sherpa
go round and round.

Watch the cutthroats pace outside
the town hall, bent on intrigues that
pull the rug from under you all

Because you failed to lift it up to
see if the floor was indeed
solid. Honest men will fit on a single lot.

Koon Woon

Love me when I am old

No need to love me when I am young,
because I can only love myself then.
No need to kiss me under the apple bough,
as any pair of fair arms would me arouse.

But love me, love me when I am old,
when the extremities of me grow cold,
when neither food nor drink will do.
For all the years that we drift through,
pretending we each other didn't know,
now love me, love me as we stand in snow

Cityscape with Solitary Figure

Not a sparrow is yet up, nor the milk trucks.
Even to malign him, the street lamps are frugal.
He who is under the shadow of the building, a deeper shadow.
He who hauls his house on his back.
Must we avoid acknowledging him?
He whose going does not make an arriving.

In the darkness he is white, brown, or black –
No one can tell or would tell.
He knows the various grids of the city and how far
Into the morning before he can get a free cup of coffee.
The park benches are partitioned
And signs saying no camping. What a life!

Formerly there was shelter from the rain
Beneath the bridge, but the stench of graffiti
Forced him to brightly-lit doorways before dawn.
Merchant-hired security sweeps him
Up in the morning and he goes as a lump
Of coal in the snow, going just for the sake of go.

The High Walls I Cannot Scale

[With apologies to Du Fu]

Desolate in my Chinatown morning
among the scraps and people sleeping in urine
doorways, I ache from the politics of the heart.

Pigeons flock together in Hing Hay Park,
no children to greet them.
I walk for my sanity, since alone in my room
before dawn, the mind constructs improbable things.

The city is humming for profits,
and I wait for the porridge place to open:
a bowl of sampan porridge
adorned with a clump of watercress.

The Chinese and I are one, scattered
to the four corners of the globe.
I have only enough to pay for one bowl,
and so, my friend, I am sorry, I must dine alone.

Gooks Who Become Geeks

My assemblage of bones and pain
Brittleness and age
That higher cognition had forced me to
Books that had to be read,
Must be read
Even as the tongues diverge
And rivers fork, never knowing
When meaning will creep from the deep.

Take that other path, some joke,
Do sociology or psychology
Instead of forestry and study diverged woods.
And if the grass wants wear,
Make a hula-hoop.
The road will inevitably get you there,
Even as the geometry twists and shouts,
So look before you leap,
For crying out loud.

If you feel betrayed, for heaven sakes,
Write another essay! Explain all the roots that toot,
The sleep you missed while lost in the tome,
While your more astute classmates,
Contemplate the erection of a missile shield.
They are not Anglo nor Saxon;
They are Asiatic. Yes, they were hidden,
As Ann Frank was hidden – up in the attic.

They are rattling their abacuses,
Positioning their slide rules.
Indoors they stayed because of the New England frost.
They studied math and actually found all the odds
That one is likely to face the moment one is born.

For this reason they did not venture far,
They waited for the roofer come to fix the leaks.
By then, they've lost their *angst*. They were geeks.

I've told you the fragility of my love…

I've told you of the fragility of my love,
and yet how it endures like a leaf pressed into a book,

how the pain and how inappropriately the hate,
like the Nagasake and Hiroshima bombs

left a silence whereof no man can speak…
It is this that is the fragility of my love,

Knowing my awareness is pain; I leave you in my mind
the many times I think of the silence

wherein my mother's voice should drone, but
the gentle hands released me to bed where the smell of
kerosene

from the village lamp burnt past the hour of moths
when we shut the window to village crickets,

when the tender bamboo shoots, their new fragile leaves bud
in the fragility of my love for you,

as I want to travel blind with you as far into the night
until the sun rises in Japan, and I will sail my junk

into phantom waters. Yet my love endures
like cloth flapping in the wind…

Two Persimmons Side by Side

Green was the lily pad on which sat the frog,
and crimson was the light through an orange sky...
Things will be all right, this night and other nights.
I am not the most gifted, nor am I the most favored;
yet I too want to flee into your arms enamored.
I have a twin in the metropolis, high in a tower,
Half-buried in the chatter of calculating machines –
he never looks back at the village
where his brother re-digs another ditch
and sighs at his long slender fingers
that might have caressed a violin...

Somewhere in the world, two
Persimmons sit side by side on a shelf,
Ripening quietly through quiet days.
On some day of some month, all guitars will weep,
and the persimmons' red hues will deepen and deepen.
For every brother there is a brother,
and for every persimmon there's another persimmon,
but for every boy is there a girl?
And for every girl is there a promised world?
No one knows except the crimson sky
and the red, moist persimmons...

Lychee

When a woman refuses your gifts,
She's a woman in the next tenement room,
And she knows you have nothing
Nor ever had anything to give her.
And you may be an emperor,
But the palace guards don't obey you,
And is this place a palace or a prison?
On her way to the communal toilet, she looks past you,
Her eyes vacant, registering nothing, and you ask,
"Is there a man on her mind? Or a job? Or a woman?"
And she is clothed in a coarse red shirt,
The one you gave her that once
Belonged to your brother, the lawyer –
She looks like the juicy meat of a lychee in winter,
Fetched by fast chariots from a far-away province.
She walks, never touching,
Though you've lived for so many years in adjacent rooms,
And water, when running in one room, can be heard in the
other.
Her hair blower hums a forlorn tune against
The soft murmurs of a city in sleep, in fornication.
The blower hums,
"I shall never marry; I shall never marry…"

Coming Are the Days…

Perfect weather in the onset of autumn
with maples turning three or four shades…
The luxury of a sun slanting
while the city is still tourist-heavy
with vine-ripe grapes bunching as in families
and the wine on tables telling
full and round stories.
And so I ask myself –
Will I ever go to Paris
and sit at a sidewalk café
and tune my poetry as I would a guitar?
Whatever the tune,
the earth is beginning to spin,
wheat- and apple-heavy
toward a golden harvest,

then toward winter.

Conveyor Belt

I've got to get past this logjam to
trade delusions on the common market.
I've got to chug along, to smoke and squeak
Into thousands of households.
More needed than Dutch cleanser,
more desired than perfume,
the perfect gift,
grits for kids,
even a thigh bone for the family dog.
Consumers,
I come along:
I am the Provider,
alms for a listless day,
folk remedy for a rainy afternoon.
I compact the garbage
I get you online
I remove unwanted hair
I am the solution
I am affordable
I am death on the installment plan
I am sugar
I am ashes
I am a promise
I am the choir in heaven
I will get you there.